Sam,
Thank you for

9/6/12

Do Right
Do Good

JEAN ALERTE
AND ZANGBA THOMSON

Cover Design by Bang

Photography by Jonathan Ortiz

Please visit www.DoRightDoGood.com for information regarding tour dates, bookings, and speaking engagements of Jean Alerte and Zangba Thomson.

To my wife, Gayna Samuel-Alerte, thank you for allowing me to keep my dreams fresh. Je t'aime. To the memory of Julian Casimir, my grandfather, thank you for that smile—your legacy lives on! And to Robert "Sha" Dunn, thank you always for watching over us.

Contents

Foreword

Why anyone would choose to live a hum-drum, mediocre life has always been a puzzle to me, and, here's why. Several weeks ago, as I prepared to catch another flight to another city from Atlanta's Hartsfield-Jackson airport, I received a phone call that literally placed me in a land that few people have traveled. Somewhat apologetically, my wife knew that I would probably want to respond to this message immediately. Calling from Williamsburg, New York was a dear friend, Jean Alerte, requesting that I write the foreword to his new book, Do Right, Do Good. Without hesitation, I told Jean that I would be honored. And now you, the reader, can begin to honor yourself by fully implementing Jean's rich wisdom and embarking on a journey to personal and financial success.

Each year approximately fifty thousand manuscripts find their way to an editor's desk and are eventually published. I estimate that if you searched long enough you will find nearly fifteen thousand different titles in the store where you purchased this book. And yet, of all the books you could be reading, you are holding Do Right, Do Good. Fate, luck, chance, coincidence?

I don't believe so. Nothing is coincidental. I am convinced that many times in the course of our lives; the Creator challenges us to be more and to do more than what we thought possible. I know nothing of your particular circumstance, whether you are young or old, male or female, rich or poor. I do know, however, that you are in search of a better life—increased wealth, health, and personal fulfillment. What this book is about to reveal has been known by only a fortunate few. Ironically, the keys contained within have evaded both the educated and the illiterate, not to mention the least, the last, and the lost. Contained within this biographical self-help guide are powerful tools that you can use, not only to construct a new life, but to improve the lives of others, as well as how to turn your dreams into reality. In the pages that follow, you will learn how to develop the "life-changing habits" of an individual who, from a standing start, built a successful and thriving business in the teeth of a down economy, and who guides and mentors others to do the same.

By reading and reviewing Jean Alerte's example and range of experiences, you, too, will be able to move from rags to riches, from breakdown to breakthrough, and from garage to greatness. You will learn how to organize your personal life in such a way that you will achieve all of your goals and objectives faster than you ever imagined. But I must warn you. You must listen with an open heart and an open mind and be prepared to act. All the noble thoughts, well intended plans, and keys to personal enrichment are of little value unless they are placed into action. To begin a journey such as this requires an act of faith. The faith to accept new thoughts, new ideas and concepts that will enable you to not only grow in every dimension but to preserve your emotional well-being long into the future.

You are unique. No one suggested that you accept this challenge; by listening to the still voice within you took the first step. What you seek, seeks you. So now I challenge you to not only use this touchstone for the next thirty days, but the remainder of your life as well. How you and I react or fail to react determines the course of our future. Trust me. Your faith will be rewarded.

Thank you, Jean, for allowing me to perform the first task on my quest to do right by doing good.

Dennis Kimbro, Ph.D.
Author, Think & Grow Rich: A Black Choice

Preface

"Always do right—this will gratify some and astonish the rest." This famous quote by Mark Twain reminds me of my mother every time I come across it. Several years ago when I was a teenager on the verge of becoming a man, and around the time when I entered the mortgage-banking and real estate business, my mother offered me advice regarding my new profession. It may have been women's intuition, but she knew all about the traps that surround lucrative businesses like real estate, and she also knew the love that I have for having the finer things in life. After putting those two factors together, she realized that she had to say something to prepare me for my future vocation. When the time was right, she pulled me aside one day and, strictly and firmly, said to me in her thick French accent, "Always do right by people and never take from anyone in a dishonest way! You know your father and I are here for you, so if there ever comes a time in your life when you are in desperate need of money, remember my advice to you today. Come to me, and either your father or I will give you the money or support that you need!"

Those powerful words revolutionized my way of thinking and gave me an enormous boost of self-confidence. I suddenly felt secure knowing that the two people responsible for bringing me into this world had my back unconditionally. Now when I look into the rearview mirror of my recent past, I can honestly say that my parents' contributions and continuous efforts in being responsible for my sister and me shaped us into the individuals that we are today. That good upbringing enabled me to always do right to everyone that I have come or will ever come into contact with.

I started writing loans at the age of eighteen. At that time the real estate business was booming; money was pouring in. Although I was by no means wealthy, I was enjoying life and the rewards that came with it. It would have been extremely easy for me to take advantage of my clients like the handful of predator lenders out there writing faulty loans. But unlike them, and being cut from a different cloth, I chose to live an honest life. I was able to avoid the temptations that my mother had warned me about by always doing right by people. I didn't prey on my clients' lack of knowledge regarding mortgage loans; instead, I educated them about it. I treated each one of them fairly by never overcharging them and giving them full disclosure of my fees and services. I had no secret motives to dishonestly acquire my clients' hard-earned money.

I also didn't favor one class of people over another. I never cared about a person's position in life or how much money they made. (Minor stuff like that has never interested me.) In the building where I worked, I treated the janitors and the corporate executives the same way that I treated my co-workers and family. I knew that if I did right by people, the Universe would also do right by me. I strongly believed the Creator would greatly bless my going forth and my coming in if I continued on the path of righteousness. No matter if I was healthy or sick, I always tried my best to do right by people. I treated everyone how I wanted to be treated—do unto them as I would have them to do unto me. I believed every individual, regardless of who they are, should abide by this simple rule.

I never became rich as a mortgage banker, but more important, I never had to ask my mother or father for money because I never treated my clients dishonestly. I always stuck to a code of ethics, and by doing so I made an honest living.

A couple of years later, I was promoted to business development manager at the company where I worked. One day while updating our business-card design, a slick idea flashed in my mind. I encouraged all our loan officers to give me a personal quote dear to him or her that represented them as a person. After gathering all of their quotes, I put each officer's quote on his or her respective business card.

When it was time for me to find a quote for my card, the Mark Twain quote that started this preface was a perfect fit. "Always do right—this will gratify some and astonish the rest." I said to myself—this is me! The quote explained how I'd been handling my business affairs, it reminded me of the timely advice that my mother had given me prior to going into real estate, and it also represented how I was raised as a kid. It wasn't just another sentence in between quotation marks. To me it meant much more than that. After taking my time and considering it carefully, I saw its true purpose in my life. It became very clear to me. I realized that if I always did right—no matter what—a few people might be pleased by my actions, but the majority of them would be too surprise by it to even acknowledge it. A few of them would see my kindness as strength, but many would view it as a weakness. This is just human nature, or human error, as some people might call it. However, I believe we should always do right.

Here's a perfect example of always doing right. Let's say early in the morning on your way to work, you are walking ahead of a total stranger. Both of you are en route to get coffee from a well-known fast-food establishment. You open the entrance door and hold it open for that stranger. But in return he walks past you without acknowledging your polite act. Embarrassingly you are left holding the door like an underpaid doorman, thinking to yourself, *why did I just hold the door for that inconsiderate person?* You could have been first in line at the register if you would have let the door go. But you didn't. You weren't selfish. You did the right and selfless thing for someone. The direct result of doing right seemed like a total disappointment at first, but in actuality the Universe appreciated it. You just helped the world to become a better place to live in, and in due time, the Universe will repay you for doing that one right thing.

On another day, let's say the following morning, you open the same entrance door and hold it for a beautiful lady. To your surprise, she acknowledges your kind act by saying, "thank you!" Immediately you feel the rewards of your kindness and you smile broadly. You feel good about doing right.

Both of these examples capture the essence of this book. In life you are going to come across people who will appreciate the things you do for them and others who will not. But no matter what people's reactions are to your kindness, always continue to do right by them. The rewards received for your continuous efforts in right doing will be priceless. You will begin to get past the biggest obstacle in your life, which is yourself. I cannot stress enough the reason why it is vital to always do right. The bible says, "if your enemy is hungry, feed him; if he is thirsty, give him something to drink, and in doing so, you will make him feel guilty and ashamed." Sometimes doing right will not only be beneficial to you but also to others.

Let's say one day you say "bless you" to someone who has just sneezed. That person might be going through a rough period in his or her life, and your kind words might help to brighten their day a bit. Your words might make that person feel loved. Doing right has that special ability of touching people lives. One of the main reasons I wrote this book was to do just that—to cast an always-do-right spell over the entire world.

Ever since I was eighteen years old, I've had numerous speaking engagements, lecturing students at different schools around the New York City area. One thing that I've noticed from being a motivational speaker is that my words have the ability to inspire people. I feel compelled by my spirit to release my motivational messages not just through speaking but also through literary, audio, and visual formats with hopes of reaching a worldwide audience. But if I can touch just one kid's life for the better—I win! I will have accomplished everything that I set out to accomplish with this book. So in a way, this is me giving back to the kids who will never get the opportunity to see me speak in public.

Always doing right is something everyone with a vision of being successful should practice daily. By doing right continually, you will develop a habit of *always* doing right. Most people think that they are only going to do right by the people who have done right by them, or they are only going to do right if they can get something out of the deal. If there is no reward, they will choose not to do right by others. That negative thinking will only hinder the best of us from fulfilling our visions. A selfish person has no real future in a selfless Universe. You won't get very far in life or in the business world with that negative attitude. It just won't happen!

You have to give before you can receive anything of great value, and when you give, give wholeheartedly. People are not stupid; they can sense if someone is either fake or authentic. If you're going to give something to someone, give it with the hope of seeing that person excel and with the joy of witnessing that wonderful moment. You too will experience happiness and growth. Never use people to move yourself higher up on the ladder of success. Do right, do good, and success will follow you all the days of your life!

When you sincerely do right by people, miracles will happen in your life—even when you don't expect them. They might happen a month later or a year later, but they will happen. Doors that were once closed will now be opened for you. The Universe has a funny way of rewarding us for doing right but has a strict way of paying us back for doing wrong. Therefore I highly recommend that if you plan on staying in the green and far away from a lot of red ink, consistently practice doing right, and in return, the Universe will always do right by you.

When I was working at a bank, there was a client of ours named Robert Standfast. In the course of me doing right by him over a long period of time, he took a certain liking to me and became my mentor. He taught me how to become a successful businessman, giving me the tools that I have used to become successful. When it came time for me to build my mortgage-banking career the way I wanted to, it was my friendship with Robert that helped me succeed. I remember him saying, "You're going to need to know how to play golf!" Golf? I was puzzled. But because I looked up to him so much, I agreed without any objections, and he began to teach me how to play. He took me to the driving range and even let me use his clubs. I felt great! I felt appreciated! Driving those golf balls down the fairway gave me a sense of power that I had never experienced.

After several lessons Robert took me to the store to buy my own equipment. But why was I being rewarded? The answer lay in how I treated Robert when he would come into the bank two years prior. I always did right by him, and he was just reciprocating. He genuinely wanted to see me grow into a successful businessman, and that's why he invested quality time in me. He didn't have to do what he did. He just did it. He took me to his private country club, and there he spent countless hours tutoring me about golf. He showed me how to hold the club correctly, how and where to strike the ball, and the purpose of each club. For my twenty-fifth birthday present, he took me to play my first nine holes. I could feel the adrenaline running through my body right down to my new pair of golf shoes. I recall feeling like I looked like a young Tiger Woods.

I appreciate every moment that I spent with Robert because he is genuinely a good person. He showed me what a real relationship is all about. At that time he owned a title company, and we did right by each other. I referred him title business, and in return he gave me mortgages. That became our business relationship. A few of my past accounts, the real estate agents, lawyers, and other people that helped my business grow, was a direct result of knowing Robert. He knew that the game of golf would give me the structure that I needed to advance my career, and because of him, I see myself treating every situation or business decision as if I'm playing on the golf course. He made it possible for me to come along with him to play in a real golfing environment, at the country club—a place I couldn't go to because I didn't have a membership. He took me there as one of his own and showed me how to play the game. So from the bottom of my heart, I would like to say thank you, Robert! Now I go and play golf with different clients and colleagues. I also teach people in my inner circle how to play golf and the importance of it.

Two important people that were very influential in my life were Robert Flower and JoAnn Monroe. They taught me practically everything I needed to know about a strong work ethic, and I very much appreciate the both of them for that. I learned by example from watching Robert and JoAnn conduct their daily business. Robert showed me some of the keys to triumph as an entrepreneur. He taught me how to keep my integrity while doing business, and how to be a great person and role model. Every day I saw him work ridiculously hard. In fact, he was so determined to succeed and to win that he competed in the 2011 Ironman competition.

When I first met Robert, he was in his late twenties and owned his own bank. He had a big corner office, and years later when he promoted me to vice president, that became my office. Robert had a lot of good qualities about him that rubbed off on me. He always carried a smile on his face and hardly got upset. To really get him mad you had to do something drastically wrong. Which nobody did. Robert gave me the opportunity to bring in new business accounts. He taught me how to nourish relationships and how to build rapport with different types of people. He taught me how to structure good loans that were beneficial to both our clients and us. With his guidance I was able to make my clients enjoy the mortgage-loan process. JoAnn on the other hand, guided me through the loan process, and taught me the core value of customer service. They will always be like family to me. They gave me my start as a mortgage banker. I consider Robert a brother and Joanne a sister. They have supported me with everything that I have done in my life, and I am thankful to them for that.

My mother is the main person in my life that has always done right by people, and she instilled that attitude in my sister and me. I witnessed the results of her right doing countless times while growing up as a kid. I remember whenever she was ever in need, our phone wouldn't stop ringing because people would constantly check up on her. They were always there to help us in our time of need because whenever they were in need of something, my mother was there to help them out. She taught my sister and me to never be selfish because selfish people always ended up alone. "No one wants to do business with a selfish person," she always said to us, "because if you only think about yourself, when it's time to do business with people, they will not trust you. And if they can't trust you— what else do you have?" I will always be grateful to my mother for telling us to always do right.

I always try to put people first by helping them out however I can. For example, whenever my company, Alerte, Carter, and Associates, throws a red carpet event, I discipline myself to always smile and listen to what people have to say before talking about my company or me. When I needed support while putting together my first comedy show, all those people that I had helped beforehand supported me without hesitation. Everyone. I helped them unconditionally and they returned the favor—I didn't even have to ask for help. They just said "Jean, let me know what you need." Or, "Jean, give me a stack of flyers so I can hand them out for you." "Give me some posters so I can hang them up in my barbershop." "Tell me how you want me to get the word out on the radio." "Let me help you get Kevin Hart on television." No one ever asked me for money because of all the things that I had done for them over the years. They remembered me helping to push their projects through my outlets. I learned that it all comes down to networking, and proper networking is all about doing right by others.

Every relationship is a give and take. Some people are wealthy, some are poor, and the rest fall between them. Even though the wealthy person might not need money from you, that doesn't mean they don't want anything from you. They might simply need your company and want to have a pleasant conversation with you. It's not always about money. There are people who just want to take-take-take without giving anything in return. That's one of the biggest problems plaguing the world. Takers! They are responsible for depleting our energy and resources. They fail to realize that giving and taking is a two-way street. You have to give before you get. That's an unbreakable rule and also one of the keys to success. You can't expect anyone to give you anything of great value without you first giving something of great value to the world. In this Universe, in whatever business you're into, no one is going to invest in you until you invest in yourself. In the beginning, you're not going to get those big-time investors with the huge checks or corporate sponsors. But if you continue to move forward toward your vision, your vision will move forward toward you.

People are attracted to successful people's hard work and dedication. That's what people love. A clear example of that would be when I was pitching the Kevin Hart comedy show to people, trying to get them to sponsor my event. No one wanted to do it for two reasons. First, they didn't know me because I didn't have a track record for producing concerts. Second, not everyone at the time had heard of Kevin Hart. So they would say if it were Chris Rock, they would do it. I didn't have Chris Rock. I had Kevin Hart, Tony Rock, and Wil Sylvince—a great line-up. I was told no many times but never got discouraged. I didn't quit, but independently I kept on pitching my comedy show idea. My team and I touched many people with our marketing efforts. We mailed out thousands of postcards to people's residences. We appeared on television to get the word out, all at our own expense. Now I look back and imagine all the money sponsors would have made if they had invested in my show from the beginning. They would have tripled their investment. But because they didn't know about me or didn't believe I could pull it off, I had to do it myself. I believed in my vision, and my team also believed in my vision. Now after my first comedy show got sold out, we have sponsors crawling out of the woodwork, calling us to say that they are interested in being a part of our future events. Amazing! That would have never happened if we didn't invest in ourselves first. If there's a reality show that you want to produce, I suggest that you pick up the camera and start recording the show yourself or find a team of people who have a similar vision to help you out. Don't expect a network to pick you up if you don't do the groundwork. After filming the pilot episode for your show, create a personal website or put it on YouTube. Promote it, and after probably getting a million views, a network might pick you up. But let them come to you first—don't go to them! When they come to you it means that you're worth more.

Chapter 1

The Power of Vision

As a kid growing up I wanted to become a CPA or something related to finance. I found out at an early age that I was actually great at math and loved dealing with numbers. The possibilities of solving numeric or algebraic equations intrigued me. One day, an adviser dear to me, seeing that I possessed strong leadership qualities, introduced me to an after-school program called Delta Epsilon Chi Activities (DECA), which is a national organization for college students who are preparing for careers in marketing, merchandising, or management. Immediately I fell in love with all the programs at DECA. I was taught how to become a successful leader and how to make informed career decisions. I was introduced to sales, marketing, hotel management, department-store retailing, merchandising, marketing, finance, advertising, and a host of other work-related fields. I learned how to successfully operate a store. DECA really opened me up to being an entrepreneur. When I saw how I interacted with customers, who were my fellow classmates, I began to see that working alongside people came very easy to me. I was a natural people person. Every day I came into the classroom with a huge smile. I was thirsty to learn and hungry for knowledge. I worked very hard and made sure that my group had enough cookies, juice, and supplies. I took my training courses very seriously as if I were really operating a business. Although I didn't plan on owning a merchandising store, I definitely knew that I wanted to run my own business, and be my own boss. Call my own shots. DECA gave me the early education and experience that I needed to turn my visions into reality, and ever since then, I have always put myself into leadership positions.

I love doing what I want to do, when I want to do it, and not being told what to do. By no means am I justifying that working for someone is a bad thing, because it's not. Everyone at some point and time in his or her life, for the simple purpose of learning, has to work under someone with superior knowledge. At many different stages of my life I too had to work for people. Therefore, you must become a follower before you can lead a team. The horse must come before the cart and not the other way around if you want to be successful.

I remember the first major vision that I had was to create a company that would help people achieve their visions—help them have a lasting impression on the world, and in 2007, with the help of a few like-minded individuals, that vision was made possible. The company is called Alerte, Carter, and Associates (ACA)—a boutique public relations and marketing agency. You see that's the funny thing about visions. By me accomplishing my vision, I put myself in a position to make a living by helping other people accomplish their vision. I love what I do because when my clients win, I win. My team wins. We are all in the business of helping people win. I want to leave behind a legacy showing that ACA was a part of building many careers and branding many different names and products to the public. I want us to be remembered as the reason why struggling companies rise high beyond expectations and became brand names like Coca-Cola, Pepsi, or Nike.

This is my vision for my company, and I believe my team feels the same way. At ACA we have Tamar Bazin, a great publicist who works extremely hard for her clients. She knows everything there is to know about public relations. She's simply amazing. Then we have Jonathan Sykes and Jason Sykes; together they handle all the marketing and events. Words can't explain their day-to-day contributions to the company. I can never forget them. They started with me from the very beginning and stuck it through with me unconditionally. I believe because we shared the same vision—the same mindset—we were able to persevere through tough times. Now together as a unit we are unstoppable because we never gave up. I remember there were times when all seemed lost. Nothing was going our way. The light at the end of the tunnel that we were traveling on got dimmer and dimmer every time we took a step toward accomplishing our vision. We could have easily quit and gone on to pursue easier careers. But we didn't. Every time life threw us a curveball we didn't get discourage. We worked harder at perfecting our swings and eventually got so good at public relations that life started to throw us easier pitches to hit. Our batting averages skyrocketed at that point. We understood the golden rule all champions abide by when pursuing a certain goal: that winners never quit and quitters never win. So in our minds, we knew we wanted to win, and that's what we ended up doing. We had traveled far away from our starting point in life. Now whenever one of our clients walk through our office doors and thank us for all the hard work and effort that we have put into branding them, or for making their event a success, it makes us feel extremely important and happy to know that we have done our jobs correctly. Our success story shows that we are indeed true visionaries.

I believe everyone, if they don't already have a vision, will have a vision one day. It might come to you while you are asleep, through your dreams, in the shower, while you are walking your dog, or early in the morning while you are driving to work. No matter what, through the course of your life, one or many visions will appear to you. You might see yourself as a doctor, a trial lawyer, or a kindergarten teacher. The possibilities are endless. I suggest the first time you envision anything worthwhile to write it down so you don't forget it. Focus on that vision as if you are babysitting a newborn baby. Never lose focus of it. Remember it needs your nurturing before it can grow. You were chosen to be its guardian. Therefore cherish it with all your heart because if you don't, you will lose focus, and your vision will become blurry. You can always correct that by simply refocusing your attention on your vision and seeing it through to the end. But it won't be easy. There are many distractions out there in the world that will cause you to lose focus.

It is very important for you to remain focused. It helps when you fine-tune your visions by creating a master plan or a blueprint for its achievement. Start the plan by saying to yourself, these are the steps that I need to take to accomplish my vision, and this is how I'm going to accomplish each of these steps. I will stick to the plan through any obstacle. This is what I'm going to do. This is what I was called to do. This is what I was put on this earth to do. You have to have faith and believe in yourself. Remember, faith is the substance of things hoped for and the evidence of things not seen. So don't let anyone stop you from dreaming or tell you that you can't do it. Just do it. Go for it. It's that simple.

Sometimes a person's vision may lie dormant because they haven't acted upon it, and an outside source like myself, through this book, might be able to awaken their vision and bring it back to the surface of their mind. This tells me that our visions never really go away. Once we envision them, they remain with us forever and will always find a way into our minds until we act upon them. Take me as an example. Ten years ago if someone would have told me that I would be writing this book, I wouldn't have believed him or her. I remember when the coauthor of this book, Zangba Thomson, who was a client of mine at the time, said to me, "Jean, I think you should write a book." My reply to him was, why? What am I going to write a book about? And he said to me, "about you, your story, and your life!"

At that moment a seed was planted in my mind. Others after him have also told me to write a book. I believe all along the Creator has been speaking to me through different people, but at the time I didn't want to listen to what he had to say. I was being stubborn. Now the voice of that vision has apparently gotten so loud inside my head that I had no choice but to act upon it. That's what visions will do. If you pay them no mind, they will constantly fight to get your attention. They mean no harm and are there just to help you grow. You have to realize that your visions are bigger than who you are. They may seem small today, but after reaching their full potential, they can become overwhelming. If you have a vision that you are passionate about, don't let it go to waste because when you're past your prime; you will regret doing so. Accomplish your visions while you still have the strength to accomplish them. Many unfulfilled visionaries say things like this: I would have done this and done that, but I didn't have the money to finance my dream. I had a baby. I had to work two jobs to support my family. I went to jail and my plans were derailed. Whatever the case may be, there shouldn't be any excuses why you didn't fulfill your vision. We all will encounter temporary defeat on our road to success, but that shouldn't stop us from reaching our destination. We will all have obstacles to overcome, but the difference between those who overcome them and those who don't is simply this: no matter what, those who overcome will always see their visions through to the end, and the underachievers will always quit somewhere along the way by making excuses. Remember, no one was born at the finish line. Everyone begins at a starting point. The privileged among us may have a monetary advantage, but we all have the same kind of willpower to persevere and finish our respective races.

Two things to look out for are fear and doubt. These two evil twin-sisters are there to hold you back from fulfilling your vision. The best way to defeat them is to wholeheartedly believe in yourself and the vision that the Creator has inserted into your mind. Believe that you are great, and you will accomplish great things. Believe in what you're doing, what it is that you have to do, and you're going to achieve it.

I remember one day I was looking back at all my earlier promotional accomplishments that I had achieved with my friends in regards to throwing local events—from college parties to club parties—and I realized that we were very successful at doing it. And during my moment of clarity, I envisioned myself producing a huge concert. It puzzled me at the moment because I hadn't done anything that major before. I didn't know where to start, but I knew that I didn't want to do the typical rap concert like everyone else was doing. I wanted to produce something totally different—something that reflected who I was as a person, and that special something was comedy. So what I did was every single day I spoke my concert vision into existence by reciting a mission statement that I had written down.

Vaguely, it went something like this: I will produce a comedy concert—no matter which obstacle may be thrown my way. I will not quit but will continue on until my vision is fulfilled. Every which way and every day I will get better and better. Of course everyone's mission statement will be different. That's expected. So tailor make your mission statement to fit your vision. I highly recommend saying your mission statement out loud, every day, to yourself, because in actuality what you're doing is convincing yourself that you will accomplish it. You see, repetition builds faith and the stronger your faith is, the easier it will be for you to fulfill your vision. And another thing, don't just keep your vision to yourself. Put it out there in the Universe. Talk about it. Tell every positive person that you know what you're planning to do. Their inputs will be very helpful. But beware—don't tell your vision to anyone negative because they might deter you from fulfilling it. Only discuss it with positive people that are going to encourage you.

The first positive person I told about my comedy show idea was my wife, my biggest supporter and my partner in life. She has always believed in me, my projects, and has supported me in everything that I do. I love her dearly for that. She loved the comedy show idea and told me that it would be successful. After that boost of confidence, I told my business partners, and they all wanted to know which comedian I was going to get to headline the concert. Truthfully, I didn't know what to tell them. I wasn't prepared for that line of questioning. I started to consider many comedians out there. I wanted to get a person who wasn't already in the limelight because I wanted to sell out my comedy show strictly on my own strengths and not because of a big name comedian. I remember later on that weekend, during a snow blizzard, my wife and I attended a show at Caroline's Comedy Club, located in Times Square in New York City. I couldn't believe how packed the club was. Somehow the bad weather didn't hinder people from coming out for a few laughs. And they weren't disappointed either. Each stand-up comedian was electrifying, and everyone in the audience had a wonderful time. I was in the right place at the right time. Ideas about my vision kept popping into my head. My self-confidence growing, I was psyched to see a room filled with people and started to believe that I could do the same thing.

There was a hunger inside of me to take my vision to the next level. At the end of the show, when my wife and I were leaving, comedian Wil Sylvince came up to us and gave me a flyer. After looking at the advertisement, I excitedly revealed to him that I wanted to produce a comedy show, and I wanted him to be a part of it. We exchanged numbers, and I told him I was going to give him a call. In a nonchalant way he replied, "Okay, sure." I could sense that he didn't believe that I was going to call him. He probably heard that type of offer countless times with nothing ever materializing from it. It was true that while telling him this, I had no venue or knowledge of putting together a big-time show. Staying true to my word, though, I ended up calling Wil a week later.

During our conversation I asked him which comedians did he think we could get for the show. He replied that he had access to top comedians, which was great! I told Wil that I wanted Kevin Hart to headline my comedy show, and in no time he gave me Kevin's management information. We ended our phone conversation on a high note.

I went over and talked to one of my colleagues and immediately he was cool with the idea. From that moment on I kept in contact with Kevin's management team, but it wasn't easy convincing them to give me a chance. The one thing that kept hindering me from being accepted by them was that I had never produced a comedy show. At the time, they knew that Kevin's career was on the way up, so they didn't want to take any chances. Imagine if they gave me a shot and the show bombed. That error on their part would have been disastrous for Kevin's career. They were just trying to protect their asset from flopping in New York. I knew I had my money in place, so I spent the next two months e-mailing and calling them constantly. I was ready to play, and they didn't want to deal me the cards to play with. It didn't take long for me to see that I wasn't getting anywhere with them, so I took destiny into my own hands and made a bigger move.

I changed my tactics. Waiting for them would have cost me my vision. I knew I had to keep moving to fulfill my vision. That's when my friends in the entertainment industry came into play. Through them I was able to set up a meeting with Live Nation. At first Live Nation didn't want to take my money. They didn't want me to lose on my investment, and they also didn't want me to tarnish their spotless image. They tried to discourage me, but I was relentless in my approach. I was so determine that I was going to win and sell out my comedy show that my vision was visible for all to see. It was alive in the room, and Live Nation began to see that. All I needed was a chance to prove myself. I was so convincing that they personally made a phone call to Kevin Hart's agent. Whatever they told him worked because the agent called me shortly afterward and told me that they were going to take a chance on me only because Live Nation was taking a chance on me. The agent then ended the conversation by saying that I had twenty-four hours to send him 50 percent of the money needed to book Kevin. I said fine. No problem. I was so excited—I signed the contract with Live Nation, sent the money to Kevin's management team, and went straight to work on my comedy-show campaign. I had no time to waste.

The first thing I did was to put up a website. I had flyers circulating all around the city. I had meetings with radio personalities and DJs to help me get the word out about the show. My team and I were out and about every day for four months straight promoting the show in the blistering cold winter. Our feet were sore and swollen, but none of us complained because we had a vision to accomplish. Because of our determination we ended up selling out the Kevin Hart Live Comedy Show at the Theatre at Westbury in Long Island, New York. Three thousand people were seated within the venue. It was such a beautiful thing to see my vision come true. I felt great. My team felt great. We were given a chance and we made the best of it. We ended up donating some of the proceeds to charity. That year alone, I ended up managing a comedy tour. Wow! After that I ended up producing another comedy show with Charlie Murphy and Tony Rock. This was the first time that Murphy and Rock had shared a stage together. I was flying on the wings of my vision. We did tons of press for the Murphy and Rock show and got them national television coverage. It was an amazing year. Now, with two successful comedic shows under my belt, I no longer get the same treatment that I got when I didn't have a resume. I went from producing my first show on my own to people wanting to be a part of my future productions.

I call those results the rewards of vision fulfillment, and although the road to vision fulfillment isn't easy; you must not lose focus by listening to the naysayers out there. Their opinions are just that—opinions. There were people out there who thought I was going to fail at producing my first comedy show because they didn't know who Kevin Hart was. At the time Kevin wasn't a household name. Now, because of the success of my comedy show, you can't say Kevin Hart's name without having a visual of who he is or heard one of his jokes. You may even be following him on Twitter or Facebook. I'm not saying that I am the person who made that happen, but I can say that I am part of his success story, which I feel great about.

Kevin acknowledges that, too. He also had a vision that he fulfilled prior to meeting me. It took him a long time doing stand-up comedy before people started recognizing him. Most of them see his recent success and think that's it. No! Kevin has been in the business for fifteen years. People believe his success came easily, but they are unaware of the hard work it took to get there. That's one thing about vision that people get mixed up. They only see the fame and fortune of a successful person. They see the result of that person's hard work and dedication and don't understand that it came about through a visionary seed that was planted in that individual's mind years earlier. The Kevin Hart of fifteen years ago isn't the same Kevin Hart that we see on television today. He has evolved from his initial starting point, I have evolved from my initial starting point, and you too will evolve one day from your initial starting point to the fulfillment of your vision.

One of the most powerful practices used rigorously by successful people is "the grind." It is something that everyone needs to do. I usually tweet Rise and Grind! Rise and Grind! I live by those words. Here's my daily routine: I get up early in the morning, run a couple of miles, have a nice breakfast, and work anywhere from eight to ten hours a day. Then I come home and spend quality time with my wife, go to sleep, and do the same thing all over again the next day. I believe you have to get up and move to become successful. The hip-hop group Outcast has a song called, "Git up, Get out!" I love this song. It embodies the soul of the grind. The chorus starts with the words, "you need to get up, get out, and get something. Don't let the days of your life pass by." Perfect! If ever there were a quote to hang on your bathroom wall, this should be it. Getting up, getting out, and getting your visions accomplished—that's the grind. Michael Jordan said it best during Nike's "Become Legendary" commercial. In an inspirational message to a group of aspiring young ballplayers standing in front of him, he says, "Maybe it's my fault. Maybe I led you to believe it was easy when it wasn't. Maybe I made you think my highlights started at the free-throw line and not in the gym. Maybe I made you think that every shot that I took was a game winner. That my game was built on flash and not fire. Maybe it's my fault that you didn't see that failure gave me strength. That my pain was my motivation. Maybe I led you to believe that basketball was a God-given gift and not something that I worked hard for every single day of my life. Maybe I destroyed the game or maybe you're just making excuses." Jordan was talking about his grind. His rise to the top. The hard work that he had put into becoming legendary. He made no excuses and fulfilled his vision.

The first thing you must do before starting your grind is to write down your vision. Writing it down holds you more accountable to accomplish that vision. The next step is to create a simple plan, maybe two to five sentences long, stating how you will accomplish your vision and when you plan on accomplishing it. Next, surround yourself with people who are movers and shakers. Seeing them doing great things will inspire you to also do great things. Don't feel different from them. You can do the same things that they are doing. The success of people like Sean Combs and Russell Simmons motivates me. I might not practice their luxurious lifestyles, but I do have one thing in common with them—the grind. We want to do better for our families and ourselves. We hustle hard so we can leave behind a great legacy. The final step is to execute your plan. That could mean anything from going to school to get a certain degree or certificate to interning at a business in your area of interest. Do whatever it is that you have to do to accomplish your vision.

To me interning offers the advantages of helping someone and getting hands-on training in the field where you want to be. The experience you get will be priceless. The grind is all about constant movement. In everything that you do, make sure that you move forward and really push toward accomplishing your vision. You have to persevere and have a fighting spirit. Boxers, for example, put themselves through a rigorous grind to stay in shape year-round. They have an intense work ethic. They beat up their bodies to prepare for bouts. It's the same thing with anyone in any occupation. To accomplish your vision, you too need to train your mind, body, and soul. You need to pray. You need to meditate. You need to put yourself in—and stay in—that mental zone where you are going to win. That's it! You have to put yourself in that one place where your vision can be realized.

There are three important people that I am fortunate to have represented at one point in time or another. These three wonderful people successfully practiced the art of grinding. The first is Alexis Diaz. I remember her strong determination to win. She had a vision of becoming an actress, so she went to school for it. She even moved to New York to pursue her acting career. She worked part-time as a bartender and networked during her spare time. And no matter what, she always kept a smile on her face. Every day we at ACA would submit her material for different projects. Eventually she was cast in many different plays, and her career took off from there. After months of being on the grind, she finally got her Screen Actors Guild (SAG) card. She never let anything or anyone deter her from fulfilling her vision. I've seen a lot of actors and actresses come and go because they didn't have the drive of the grind in them, but not Alexis. When things didn't work out for her during the first year or two, she didn't give up. She didn't choose an easier profession. No! She kept grinding, and that's why she and I worked so well together. We had the same drive. We had the same hunger to go out there and grind to accomplish our visions. It was beneficial for both of us to work together because we motivated each other to do great things.

The second person is Anthony Gurino. He is also an actor and an entrepreneur and a family man as well. His work ethic is truly amazing. If he was in New York and was suddenly told to fly out to Los Angeles for an important audition, he would do it immediately without asking any questions. Doing what he needs to do or going wherever he needs to go to accomplish his vision has been his trademark. No obstacle has ever stopped him from reaching his desired goals. He makes no excuses in life and does what he has to do to win. That's his passion. He makes the right moves and finds interesting ways to make things happen. Because of his daily grind, we at ACA were able to get him signed to one of Los Angeles's top talent agencies, Diverse Talent Group.

The third person is Patrick Jeffery, an incredible screen-writer who wrote the epic story of the first African American billionaire, *The Reginald F. Lewis Story*, which is currently in development at Paramount Pictures. With all sincerity, I must say that Patrick was the motivational force behind the creation of ACA because he was my very first client. He pushed me to become who I am. Through his overcoming life's challenges I have learned a great deal about perseverance and hard work. On the night of my twenty-fourth birthday, he was involved in a serious motorcycle accident. With sadness I went to visit him at the hospital, and his situation seemed dire. His once-cheerful demeanor had darkened severely. I thought about his family. His children. How were they coping with this tragic accident? What about his career? Most people, when faced with a life-threatening injury like his, would have stopped pursuing their dreams. But not Patrick! He kept going until he recovered. He believed in himself and believed in his vision. He went on to work on a project called *Inside Buffalo*, which is a story about the buffalo soldiers. He became one of the producers. That golden opportunity enabled him to attend a film program at Colombia University, and the rest is history.

Chapter 2

The Pursuit of Happiness

The pursuit of happiness—what does that mean? When I heard about the biographical drama film *The Pursuit of Happyness*, based on Chris Gardner's nearly one-year struggle with homelessness, I couldn't wait to see how an on-and-off homeless person would turn his life around and become a stockbroker. On opening day I was very excited; I rushed to the theater to watch it. From beginning to end, Gardner's story captured my attention. I felt empowered by it. Him fulfilling his vision made me realize that there was no reason why I couldn't fulfill mine. I went back to the theater several times after that to watch *The Pursuit of Happyness* until it became a part of me. I even have a DVD copy in my office. I play it every now and then as a reminder to never give up.

Mr. Gardner and I share many similarities. I too have invested in projects that have drained my savings. I can relate to Chris's emotions and frustrations whenever he faced temporary defeat. He had a lot of resilience, but no matter what, he was going to keep pushing until he made life better for him and his son. That was his motivation. He had to win! He didn't let the homeless shelter define who he was. No! He used it as a temporary place of refuge and started from there. He became an intern stockbroker, and months later, he was rewarded a full-time position over nineteen other competitors. Wow! He defied the odds and now owns his own multimillion-dollar brokerage firm. He is truly a role model, and his life story is something that we should all look at whenever we feel discouraged.

I remember when I first started ACA, I used to wake up early in the morning and tell my wife, "this part of my life is called running." She would laugh, but I was serious. I would leave home with a suit on, and all day I would be running around the city networking with different people from different companies, going from this event to that event meeting people that I needed to talk to. It was a pursuit. I met with so many people; the majority of them were talkers, and the rest were doers. In life, you're going to come across a lot of talkers before you meet one doer. Don't be discourage when you find yourself always meeting the talkers of the world, or what we call in my office "professional partiers." But if you keep pushing toward your vision, sooner or later you will eventually break away from the talkers and find that one doer who will help you fulfill your vision.

Happiness will be found in the *pursuit* of fulfilling your vision. I can truly say that my happiness is directly linked to the process of me fulfilling anything of value in my life. Doing the work is what makes me happy, and after completing a project I can then appreciate the paycheck that comes along with it. Yes, we do need money to live a good life, but money does not bring one happiness. Money is the reward of happiness. There's no doubt about that. When you love what you do for a living—and the process of doing it—you will become successful and make a lot of money in that profession. The treasure is in cherishing the part of your success that made you who you are today. Money didn't make you. The grind made you!

Most of the time people only recognize someone's monetary worth, and they are attracted by it. But they don't see the hard work of that person's grind. Chase what you love doing. Don't chase money because you won't get very far, and your work won't be as crisp as it needs to be. Your passion will not be in the project. It may come out good but not great. Loving the grind enables you to become great, and being great will one day put you in the same category with other great people who are also doing great things. Have a habit of being on the grind, but don't become addicted to it because too much of anything is never good. Keep a good balance between your work and your family life. Loving your grind will be the reason why you surpass others. While your competition may balk at your doing hard work, you will have fun doing it. That's the difference between those who are successful and those who are not. You will become a natural at what you do while others will be forcing it. The grind lovers will always be motivated by the grind because they love it. That's what drives them to succeed. I remember when I was in real estate, I use to love the process of selling homes, handling the mortgages, and getting my clients approved for loans. That was my love. The hard work that I put in for my clients was rewarding. When I saw the smiles on their faces after getting them a low interest rate or making it possible for them to get cash from their homes for repairs, I felt good about the job I had done. Baking the cake is the process, and the happiness in baking that cake is the icing on the cake.

I've been pursuing happiness for the last eleven years now, and I can truly say that I have put all my energy into everything that I have pursued. People recognize that and have always supported me because of my love for the grind.

I always believe in the projects I am involved with. Of course there are going to be ups and downs. For example, I remember there were times when I couldn't pay my phone bill or I didn't have the money to buy a plane ticket when I had to go to a meeting in another country. There was always one obstacle after another whenever I pursued anything of value, but when something was wrong in my life, and I was unhappy, no one knew because I always had a smile on my face. Showing that I was unhappy would have made my situation unhappy. Instead, I choose to brighten up the world by smiling or by simply telling someone hello. Every day I try to brighten someone's day, and in return, that motivates me to become a better person. It makes me feel good about myself. Today I gave away five dollars to five different homeless people that I met on the street. I don't really pick and choose how I will give back, but today it was with money. Tomorrow it might be speaking to high school students. The main idea is to give back.

There was a scene in *The Pursuit of Happyness* that opened my eyes. Chris Gardner and his son, Chris Jr., were playing basketball, and Chris Jr. made a basket. But before he could celebrate, Will Smith, who starred as Chris in the movie, told his son, "You probably going to be good like I was. That's kind of the way it works, you know. I was below average. So you'll probably ultimately rank somewhere around there. You'll excel at a lot of things but not this. So I don't want you shooting this ball around here all day and night." Wow! Chris Jr. agreed, but he also got discouraged and threw his ball away. Imagine your parents telling you that you couldn't do something that you loved doing. That would have been devastating to hear as a kid. You probably would have abandoned your dreams and would have pursued something else. But Chris, seeing the mistake that he had made, immediately felt guilty. He walked up to Chris Jr. while the boy was putting his basketball in a grocery bag and took a deep breath. He said something that I believe all parents should say to their children one day. "Don't ever let somebody tell you can't do something. Not even me! You got a dream—you have to protect it! People can't do something themselves, they want to tell you that you can't do it. You want something—go get it! Period!" I believe that was one of the greatest comebacks I've ever seen on the big screen. Chris could have left his message of discouragement linger in his son's head forever, but he didn't. He chose to do right by his son and tell him the truth. Chris was right. In life, someone will tell us one day that we can't do this or we can't do that, but don't get discouraged.

Before I started my real estate career, I remember sending out letters to people to let them know that I was a mortgage banker. Some people said that I shouldn't pursue that profession because I wouldn't excel at it. But how would they know? I valued their opinion, but I ended up disagreeing with them and kept on pursuing my career. Years later I ended up being the vice president of sales for the company that I worked for. I was happy. My pursuit brought joy to my family and me, but it wouldn't have happened if I had listened to the naysayers. So go out there and do what makes you happy. Unlock your inner tiger.

The path of the grind is not a get-rich-quick scheme, so don't be a get-rich-quick schemer. Don't fall into that trap. Nothing of value will ever be appreciated unless it is worked hard for. Take, for example, lottery winners. The majority of

them go broke within five years. They don't value their win-
nings because they didn't work hard to earn them. Whenever
people find themselves in need of money and see an opportunity to make quick money, they immediately jump on it. In the
long run, they end up losing time, which is more valuable than
the money that they were desperately seeking in the first place.
When you lose time, you can't get it back.

One of my basic rules of business is to build the business
and not the money. There's a Chinese proverb that says that a
man who treads slowly goes farther than a man who treads fast.
He who treads slowly will pace himself and won't drown. He
who treads fast will eventually get tired; his leg muscles will
eventually cramp up, and he will drown. Therefore, pace yourself in your pursuit of happiness.

Will Smith, one of my mentors from a distance, has inspired
me in so many different ways. His work ethic, and his pursuit
of happiness, is something I admire. The legacy that he is leaving behind for his family, and the opportunities he has provided
for them, is something that I also want to leave behind for my
family. It's said that Will Smith's father tore down a brick wall
in front of his business. He told Will, who was twelve years old
at the time, and his nine-year-old brother to rebuild the bro-
ken wall. At first they thought it was impossible, and why did
their father just break down a wall, only for them to repair it?
It didn't make any sense to them. But being obedient, they followed their father's instructions, and it took them a year and a
half to rebuild the wall. After becoming a successful rapper and
actor; Will remembered his wall-building experience, and said,
"You don't try out to build a wall. You don't set out to build a
wall. You don't say, 'I'm going to build the biggest, baddest,
greatest wall that's ever been built.' You say, 'I'm going to lay
this brick as perfectly as a brick can be laid.' You do that every

single day and soon you will have a wall." What an incredible statement. In pursuing your happiness you too will have to take one step at a time or accomplish one goal at a time before you can fulfill your vision. Don't rush things or try to take a shortcut to success. That will only lead to shortcomings in the business that you are pursuing. But perseverance, hard work, and dedication go a long way.

My parents have always supported me in any profession that I pursued. They are my backbone. I remember one day I came home from a long day at work, and there was a nicely dressed gentleman sitting at our dining room table. Before him was a small stack of paper and a pen. In a gentle tone I asked him why was he there? His answer surprised me. "I'm here to refinance your parent's home," he said with a smile on his face. What? I said to myself. How could my parents do this to me? Why didn't they come to me to refinance their loan? I felt betrayed by the two people dearest to me. I wanted to storm out of the dining room, but I didn't. I held my composure. I chose to compete for the first time in my life for something that I really wanted. At this time I was green and hadn't closed any mortgage deals yet. I took a deep breath and told the gentleman, "Well I'm sorry, but my parents are not going to use you to do their mortgage. Thank you but no thank you!" He stood up, grabbed his paperwork, and left.

That night, my father told me that situation was a test. If I would have allowed that gentleman to process their mortgage loan meant that I wasn't qualified to do it, but because I stepped in and took the situation into my own hands, he would allow me to do the loan. I was extremely happy. The point my father was trying to make was that life wasn't easy. You have to pursue what you want, and don't expect anyone to give you anything without you working hard for it first. I appreciated the lesson learned that day. You can't think that because it's your parents or your best friend that they have to do things for you. Nobody, regardless of blood ties or friendship bond, has to cater to your needs. Two days after bringing my parent's application into the bank, the loan officer I had sent away came back to our home with his children in his arms. He was telling my father to give him another chance because he had kids that he had to feed. My father said, "You have kids, and I have a kid also. The same way you love your children and want to support them is the same way I love my kid and want to support him. Me letting my son refinance our mortgage is me showing my support for him. If he wants to work hard for his money, I will support him!" That's it! My father stood by me that day. I appreciated him and the decision he made for me to refinance their home, and more important, he gave me my first mortgage deal. I ended up getting them a great deal. That was eleven years ago, and their interest rate is so low that no one can touch it. They will never have to refinance their home again.

Chapter 3

Surround Yourself with the Right People

A successful person is a person who sets a goal and aims to accomplish it; an unsuccessful person has no goals and doesn't know what he wants to become in life. The successful person is focused on fulfilling his vision, and the unsuccessful person sees everyone's vision but not his own. The successful person surrounds himself with the right crowd of people and succeeds, but the unsuccessful person surrounds himself with the wrong crowd of people and fails. Therefore, I believe that it's extremely important to surround yourself with the right group of people because the circle that you are within will define who you are as a person.

Your environment may be unpleasant, but it doesn't define who you are as a person. It's just a place where you are residing at the moment. You can choose to remain there or elevate to a better place. The choice is yours. Remember, it's not where you're from but where you are, and where you are mentally depends heavily on the people you choose to surround yourself with. It is written in Proverbs (12:26), "The righteous should choose his friends carefully, for the way of the wicked leads them astray." And in 13:20 it says, "He who walks with wise men will be wise, but the companion of fools will be destroyed." Wow! Those are some powerful words of wisdom. I strongly believe that anyone who faithfully abides by those words will become successful. But those who don't pay heed to wisdom will live a life filled with misery. They will come up with a million and one excuses why they haven't accomplished anything of value. But what they fail to realize is that they became failures in life because they surrounded themselves with the wrong group of people, which in turn led them to live the wrong life. Wrong things started happening to them all of a sudden. They met the wrong spouse or applied for the wrong job. Everything seemed wrong. If the right answer smacked them right across the face they would probably think it was a problem. Eventually, wrongness becomes them, and they develop a habit of always making the wrong decision. But anyone who has ever achieved anything of value will tell you that you have to make countless amounts of right decisions before you can fulfill any vision. So a person who constantly makes the wrong decision has no chance whatsoever of ever fulfilling anything of value because their wrong decisions will always lead them in the wrong direction—far away from where their visions are. It brings joy to my heart when I see an impoverished kid, against all odds; rise above his or her dire circumstances to achieve great things. They could have used their humble beginnings as an excuse not to pursue their visions, but they chose not to. They used their humble beginnings as motivation to fulfill their visions. Amazing! But in order for them to achieve that positive level of thinking, they had to surround themselves with the right group of people.

When I was a teenager I attended my first motivational seminar. The seats were filled to capacity, and some people unfortunately had to stand for hours to hear the lecture. My friend and I were positioned not too far from the podium and clearly heard the speaker say, "The friends that you have today will not be the same friends that you will have in five years if you become successful!" Immediately I had doubts about that statement. It couldn't be true. My best friend at the time was seated right next to me, and we were inseparable. There was no way that we weren't going to be best friends forever. I was so naïve. Years later when I started ACA, this statement came true. I began to spend more time on the grind. I had no time to hang out anymore because I wanted my business to succeed.

My friends respected what I was doing, and they supported me by letting me be me. Suddenly my inner circle began to change. People that I was working with became my friends because I was around them all the time. My life began to reach new heights because of my association with them. I started meeting other like-minded individuals and became success-ful. My thinking was right. I married the right woman, chose the right profession, and even bought the right car. Everything seemed right in my life, so doing anything wrong was out of the question. I eliminated every bad influence from my life. If someone had the financial means to help my company grow but was potentially a bad influence, I stayed away from that individual. I only allowed people who were doing right by oth-ers into my life. Sincere relationships only. No gimmicks. Now when I look around, everyone around me is successful in his or her own right. We might not all be in the same status as far as annual income, but we all have one thing in common—we chose to surround ourselves with the right group of people.

I strongly suggest after reading this chapter that you analyze all the people within your inner circle. Honestly ask yourself this question: do the right people, the wrong people, or a mixture of both surrounds me? The answer will determine why you're successful, not successful, or somewhere in between. If you are not a successful person, and your gravy train has derailed, I have some good news for you. The best way to get back on track is to cut ties with the wrong people in your life. Simple as that. Spend some time with yourself. Regroup. Start thinking positively. Eliminate all negative thoughts because as a man thinketh in his heart so shall he become. Build yourself up again, and the best way to do that is to surround yourself with the right group of people who will love and care about you. You don't need an army of friends. All you need is that one person or group that you can call your own.

When I was a mortgage banker, there was a kid that I knew who was heading in the wrong direction. He used to hang out with the wrong group of friends, drinking and smoking his life away. He had no goals. One day he approached me and asked me for a job, but the way he was dressed told me otherwise. After seeing his sincere determination, and the fact that he wanted desperately to change his life, I agreed to employ him. He worked about a year and a half for me before I left the real estate game to start ACA. Now that same individual who was headed down the wrong path is a successful real estate agent. He's in a committed relationship, and even has his own place, all because he decided to surround himself with the right group of people. He's not the same person that use to drink and smoke. No! He is totally different because his inner circle has changed for the better. I am so proud of him. Recently we bumped into each other, and he expressed his gratitude to me for giving him a chance. He even said that he still has the fifteen ties and dress shirts that I bought for him, and that I was his mentor. Wow!

On a personal level, surrounding yourself with the right spouse can make or break you—financially, emotionally, and even spiritually. My wife is my biggest asset and supporter. When I speak of pursuing new projects, she immediately tries to see my vision and believes that together we will fulfill that vision. Her support is priceless. I wouldn't sell it for any amount of money or trade it for any expensive goods. But my wife does not always accept every idea that I run by her. She only accepts the ones that I successfully paint in her mind. If a piece of my vision is missing after I have related it to her, then she will in turn have doubts about me fulfilling that vision, which is understandable. Therefore I try my best to describe what it is that I want to accomplish in full detail.

My wife and I communicate every single day, which is something I would not have been able to do if I had married the wrong person. The main thing that holds any relationship firmly together is communication. Without communication there is no real relationship, but it's a hard thing to do. People communicate every day, but communicating your visions to someone that you care about can be challenging. Your spouse might be tired and may not want to hear anything that day. You might not have patience and get mad at them because they aren't listening to you. But that is not the right way to win anyone over. You shouldn't get emotional. You should always show love. Your spouse should see the same type of love that you have for them in the project that you are talking about. It has to be so passionate that all they can say is, wow! You have to communicate it to them as clearly as possible. Don't be vague when describing your vision. No one will fill in the blanks. I always tell my wife that I paint the picture and then put the frame on it versus putting the frame up and then trying to squeeze the picture inside the frame.

You have to be very descriptive when describing your vision to someone. You must include the who, what, where, when, why, and finally how you are going to accomplish that vision. On the other hand, trying to explain your vision to the wrong person can be challenging. You might be in a committed relationship with someone that you truly love, but that person is totally into himself or herself and could care less about what you have to say. This type of relationship drains visionaries and poses a serious problem in them trying to fulfill anything of value. Their time is spent catering to their spouse's needs instead of pursuing their visions. Eventually they become very unhappy and their marriages fail. Divorce happens. All of this wouldn't have happened if they had picked the right person to get married to. Imagine if they had the right spouse that they could share their ideas with. Things would have turned out differently; their marriages would have blossomed. Support for each other would have been there. I was very fortunate to find a supportive woman like my wife. She's truly my biggest fan, and I appreciate everything that she has done for me. She has always been there. Sometimes I don't know what I would have done without her! She always encourages me to pursue my dreams, and I love her for that. It's rare to find a spouse that will put their dreams on hold to help you build yours. She showed me that in a relationship there are challenges and compromises. If there is ever a dream that she wants to pursue in the future, I will be there to support her unconditionally. No doubt about it.

President Barack Obama and First Lady Michelle Obama's marriage is a perfect example of why it is very important to choose the right spouse. When Mr. Obama was on the campaign trail to become president of the United States, it was his wife Michelle that made the greatest sacrifice in their relationship. Seeing that her husband needed her support, she made one of the hardest decisions in her life. Without thinking twice, she stepped down from her $273,000-a-year job with the University of Chicago Hospital to help her husband with his campaign. Wow! What an act of unselfishness. Imagine all the obstacles Mrs. Obama had to overcome before securing her position at the hospital: All the hard work and dedication that she had to put in before fulfilling her vision. All those years of schooling. To just one day say, I love my husband this much that I am willing to set aside a career that is dear to me to help him fulfill his vision.

I applaud her for that. At the time she was earning twice as much as her husband. Twice! But she had a vision. She saw the bigger picture. Change in America. She knew that vision wouldn't have been gained without her sacrifice. All those years of thinking the right thoughts and knowing that there isn't any "I" in the word "us," she eliminated her story from the equation and stood by her family. Even after her husband was elected president, she still has no intention of resuming her career at the hospital. Instead, she continues to play her role well as a mother and a wife who supports her husband unconditionally. I strongly believe that President Obama's success is a direct result of him choosing the right spouse. He picked the right woman, and when it mattered the most, she made the right decision.

Chapter 4

Do the Right Thing

I remember watching Spike Lee's *Do the Right Thing* and thinking to myself, man what an awesome movie! But the interesting thing that stood out to me was that the storyline was filled with characters that chose to constantly do the wrong thing, time and time again, just like people in the real world. The racial problem started at Sal's Famous Pizzeria, which was owned by a proud Italian American businessman named Salvatore. His pizza shop was located in the heart of an African American community, Bedford-Stuyvesant, Brooklyn, New York. On a hot summer day, while eating a slice of pizza, Buggin' Out, a African American activist, notices that Salvatore's "Wall of Fame" only has pictures of great Italian American celebrities. Immediately he gets upset and asks Salvatore, "Why isn't there any brothers on the wall here?" Salvatore replies, "If you want brothers on the wall, get your own place, and you can do what you want to do. You can put your brothers and uncles, nieces and nephews, your stepfather, stepmother, whoever you want. You see this is my pizzeria. American Italians on the wall only!" Buggin' Out is offended by Salvatore's prideful answer. "You own this," he immediately shoots back, "but rarely do I see Italian Americans eating in here. All I see is black folks. So since we spend much money here, we do have some say!" There is a few seconds of silence, and then Salvatore asks Buggin' Out, "You looking for trouble? Are you a troublemaker? Is that what you are?" Buggin' Out replies, "Yeah, I'm a troublemaker! I'm making trouble!" Salvatore grabs a bat and makes his way from behind the counter. He wants to bash in Buggin' Out's head, but his son steps in and takes the bat away. Salvatore ends up kicking Buggin' Out from his shop, but before he leaves, he poisons the other customers' minds to boycott Sal's Famous Pizzeria.

Wow! What an intense moment. I don't know about you, but this minor issue could have been avoided if both parties would have chosen to do the right thing from the very beginning. There wasn't anything wrong with Buggin' Out's probing question that Sal's Famous Pizzeria was located in a predominately black neighborhood and that most of Salvatore's customers were African American; Buggin' Out felt that out of respect for his black customers, Salvatore should have also put up pictures of great African American leaders like Martin Luther King Jr. and Malcolm X on his "Wall of Fame" alongside the great Italian American celebrities. An understandable demand, but the insulting way Buggin' Out asked his question provoked Salvatore to anger. If he had asked in a respectful manner, he would have gotten back a respectful answer. Better yet, he could have made Salvatore consider the fact that it would be a great idea to also include prominent figures within the

African American community on his "Wall of Fame." Buggin' Out missed that golden opportunity because he didn't do the right thing by asking for something the right way. On the other hand, Salvatore at this point could have been the bigger man, but instead, he took Buggin' Out's intrusive question as invading his First Amendment rights and his private space. Immediately, he disregarded the fact that Buggin' Out was one of his paying customers and defended his territory the best way he knew how. With all due respect to Salvatore, he had every right to defend his decision to put only Italian Americans on his "Wall of Fame." Would you let someone come into your home or place of business and dictate how the place should look or what you should put in it? Certainly not! Salvatore probably thought, who is this person telling me who I should put on my wall? Where was he when I was working hard, day and night, to fulfill my vision of owning a pizzeria? Did he give me any money for the construction of my shop? I don't remember his contributions at all! So why is he disturbing my peace?

Many of us would have also been offended by Buggin' Out's question. At that moment of truth, I believe Salvatore had it in his power to right the wrong that Buggin' Out had committed. I imagine if he would have taken a deep breath, eliminated all the negative thoughts floating around in his mind, and replied in a calm way by simply saying, "Buggin' Out, you know what? You have a valid point. Give me some time. Let me think about it." Immediately that answer would have disarmed Buggin' Out and would have created a good line of communication between two men from different ethnic backgrounds. That's the incredible power of doing the right thing. It is one of the greatest defensive stances a person can take while being attacked verbally by another person. But instead of doing the right thing, Salvatore grabbed his bat with the intention of doing bodily harm to Buggin' Out. From that point on in the movie, violence runs rampant. Radio Raheem ends up being choked to death by a police officer and Sal's Famous Pizzeria ends up being burned to the ground. Those horrific things wouldn't have happened if Buggin' Out and Salvatore would have chosen to communicate—to do the right thing.

In its simplest form, Karma is defined as what goes around comes back around. Do right, do good, and righteousness and goodness will come back to you in many different positive forms. But do wrong, do bad, and wrongness and a host of bad luck will come back to you in many different negative forms. It's a simple concept. But comprehending Karma takes time. In everything that we do, we have a choice to do it or not to do it. Whether it's a good idea or a bad idea, it doesn't matter; the choice is always ours to make. There's no such thing as an all-right choice or a maybe choice. Choices are either good or bad, or to be metaphysical about it, some might say that our choices are neither good nor bad. But it's the intentions of the people making the choices that decide whether a certain choice is good or bad. If you think about all the choices that you have made, you will see that where you are in life is a direct result of you doing or not doing the right thing. You will no longer blame others but yourself for you not being successful. Your visions weren't fulfilled because you didn't nurture the visionary seed that was planted in your mind many years ago. Instead, you didn't water and feed your visionary seed when it should have grown into a tree with many beautiful, blossoming flowers. You probably just didn't make the same mistakes twice, but you made them again and again until it became the norm. That's one thing about successful people; they never make the same mistakes twice.

If I see bad qualities in a potential client, I don't do business with that person because I have learned from experience not to. Maybe they haven't done anything to me per se, or haven't scarred me yet, but I would be a fool not to trust my instincts. It doesn't matter if the person has a check in his or her hand or not because bad business is bad business no matter which way you look at it. All money isn't good money. I didn't become an entrepreneur to become enslaved by money. I became my own boss to build a legacy for my family and me. I did it to be free and to provide an opportunity that would also give freedom to my employees.

One day on a brisk autumn evening, I had the pleasure of talking to a twenty-three year old barber. Our conversation went very well. I could tell that he loved cutting hair because of the excitement in his voice. But there was one obstacle hindering his growth. His parents didn't take his ambition of becoming a career barber very seriously. They were more concerned with him acquiring a college degree in finance. He appreciated his parents' input, but he didn't want to pursue a career in finance. It didn't interest him at all. He wanted to be a barber because that's what he loved doing. Too many times I have seen people do the wrong thing by choosing the wrong careers, and as a result they always ended up unhappy. Knowing this made it possible for me to advise this young man regarding the dilemma he was facing. I told him very firmly, "Do not let anyone push you toward something that you don't love doing. If you love cutting hair, then by all means you should cut hair, and while you're cutting people's hair, work on being the best barber in the world. Build your clientele, save money, and become a business by opening up your own barbershop. Hire the best barbers out there and do right by them!" I don't know where those words came from that day, but they sounded sweet coming out of my mouth. That young man appreciated every word that I said to him. Maybe no one had told him beforehand to pursue his vision, but I did, and I felt good about doing it. I could see a little light bulb sitting on top of his head. He was finally beginning to think constructively. The idea of acquiring a degree in finance no longer held him in bondage. He was free to fulfill his vision. For him, it was not about the money. It was all about him being happy doing what he loved doing, which was cutting people's hair.

Another memorable conversation I had regarding doing the right thing was between a fifteen-year-old boy and myself. Not too far into our conversation, he asked me a series of questions. "How do I deal with all the distractions that's going on around me in high school?" He asked before exhaling deeply, and without waiting for an answer, he continued, "and how do I become successful when I get older? What do I do?" I took a few seconds to think about how to answer his questions correctly. Because he was only fifteen, I didn't want to tell him the wrong thing because it would have affected him for the rest of his life. People normally ask me those same types of questions while they are attending college, not while they are in high school. I saw the intelligence inside the young man that day. I was very proud that, at a very young age, he was interested in being successful. In regard to the distractions at school, I told him to stay focused on graduating and getting into a good college. I told him to do the right thing and to make the right decisions when opportunities presented themselves. He asked, "How do I make the right decision?" I replied that every decision a person makes, if it benefits everyone involved in a positive way, is normally the right decision. He understood where I was coming from. We had the same entrepreneurial spirit living within us. I didn't have to sugarcoat anything with him—he appreciated the rawness of my message. He was focused on being successful. All he needed was for someone to tell him how to fulfill his vision by giving him the blueprint of that vision.

In fifteen minutes, I briefly explained to him every chapter of this book, and he soaked it all in. I told him to find out what it is that he loves to do. Once he acknowledges that one special thing, he should nurture it until he gets so good at it that it becomes what he does in life. It becomes his livelihood. I told him that there are many ways in identify what that one special thing is. He might go to sleep one night and dream about doing it, and when he wakes up, he might find himself doing it in real life. It could be a hobby that he has been doing since he was a little kid or a brand new love that he has just picked up. Whatever it is, I told him that special thing would never fail to bring him happiness, and if he were separated from it, his heart would stop racing. He would gasp for air because he and that special thing were in love with each other. It's like a relationship. I told him that no matter what, never let anyone deter him from doing what he loves to do. He should always stay focused. He nodded his head in agreement. We shook hands, said our good-byes, and went our separate ways. Later on that week, I learned that the young man who I had advised a few days prior was a youth counselor at an outreach program in the Bronx, New York. He spent his spare time assisting other young men his age to become successful. Wow! Fifteen years old, and he was already a leader, and more important, he chose to do the right thing every single day of his life.

Doing the right thing isn't as easy as it sounds. For example, I go through the same daily struggles just like everyone else on this planet. The right choices that I made in life put me in the position where I am today, and the wrong choices put others where they are. To illustrate this point, let's say that you and someone that you don't really know are living in the same town.

You dine at the same restaurants and order the exact same food. Every day, on your way to work, you drive alongside each other on the same highway in the exact same model vehicles. You work in the same building for different companies. It seems both of your lives are mirror images. Both of you are successful. Then all of a sudden, your supervisor approaches you and tells you that you are being promoted with a pay raise. All your hard work and dedication have finally paid off. Yes! You are excited. To celebrate, you go out with your friends to your favorite restaurant and celebrate. But at the end of all the celebration, you noticed that something seemed awkward. The person that you always see throughout the day is no longer sitting at his favorite table in the corner next to the window. This weird event causes you to think. The next day on your way to work, and several days following that, you no longer see that person driving on the highway next to you. You no longer see him when you go to the mall. You become puzzled and start saying to yourself, what happened to so-and-so? Then one day you surprisingly see a mug shot of that person on the local news. The headline reads: "Account Manager Embezzles Hefty Sum of Money from Federal Credit Union Bank!" Wow! You are in a state of shock. Then it finally dawns on you that although you had many similarities, you differ in your way of thinking. You chose to do the right thing to become successful, but that person chose to do the wrong thing to become successful. In the end, for doing the right thing—working hard for something—you got promoted with a pay raise. But that other person, because he chose to do the wrong thing, lost his job at the bank and got arrested and lost his freedom. Therefore, I strongly suggest that you practice doing the right thing because it will pay off in the long run, but if you do the wrong thing, you will be paying for it for the rest of your life!

Everyone has the ability to do the right thing. Once you come to the conclusion that you will always do right by others, your life will change for the better. When you throw out positive energy in the Universe, positive things will happen to you. If you throw out negative energy, negative things will happen to you. I read somewhere that statistics show that oftentimes drug dealers usually end up dying before the addicts that they sell drugs to. Why is that? Besides the occasional overdosing of drug users, something bad always happens to the person dealing the drugs before the person that's doing the drugs. Whether it's being in prison or being shot or stabbed, something bad will always happen to the person not doing the right thing. It's the law of the Universe. You will receive the exact same energy that you are putting out. If you're doing harm to others, guess what? Sooner or later, harm is going to come to you. Period! When I was growing up, my mother use to always help people that would ask her for help. She denied no one. Then afterward I would hear her complaining about the exact same thing that the person she had just helped complained about. That always puzzled me. I use to tell her that I didn't understand why she was helping people when she was in need of the same help. Why not help us and enjoy the little that we had? And she said, "When someone asks you for help, always try your best to help them out because in your time of need, help will also come your way. Even if it's not the same person that you helped, someone is going to help you in your time of need." Since that day I've been abiding by those wise words.

Every day when I wake up in the morning, I decide that I will do the right thing today. Maybe it's opening the door for someone or simply saying hello to a total stranger. It could even be something life changing. If I know a kid that's headed in the wrong direction, I'm going to have a talk with him or her. Me telling that individual to do the right thing can make a difference in their lives. I might be the only person telling them to do right. Maybe their parents are fed up and sick and tired of them always getting in and out of trouble. Who knows? By listening to me, they might decide to stay home and study rather than getting in trouble with their friends. The positive possibilities are endless. They will wake up to a new day and see themselves ascending while their friends are descending, all because you chose to tell them to do the right thing. Karma is going to come back to you and reward you in your time of need.

I remember watching *The Passion of the Christ*, directed by Mel Gibson. Jesus said something that stood out to me. He said to his disciples, "You are my friends, and the greatest love a person can have for his friends is to give up his life for them." What a remarkable statement. I considered it for a moment and reflected on life in general. Imagine if we all thought the same way as Jesus did. This world would be a better place to live in. I drifted back into the movie just in time to notice that not everyone felt the same way as Jesus did. Judas Iscariot, one of the twelve disciples, secretly made a deal with the chief priests and the elders to betray Jesus for thirty pieces of silver coins. Wow! Here was someone who was ready to die for him and in return he repays this person by betraying him for money. I was shocked by Judas's act of deceit. I came to the conclusion that one out of twelve people in this world has the soul of Judas Iscariot in them—people who would stab you in the back time and time again after you have continuously done right by them. But doing wrong to others comes with an expensive price to pay. When Judas saw that Jesus was condemned to die, he immediately felt guilty and returned the thirty pieces of silver coins to the chief priests and the elders. He realized that he hadn't done the right thing. An innocent man was about to die because of his wrongdoing. The chief priests and the elders paid him no mind because they already had Jesus in custody. So Judas no longer had value to them. Unable to deal with his inner demons, Judas ended up committing suicide by hanging himself. He died because he put out negative energy, and a negative thing ended up happening to him. It's important to note that Judas ended up dying before Jesus was crucified. The wrongdoer ended up giving up his ghost before the person he wronged met his preordained death. Judas didn't even get to spend his thirty pieces of silver coins.

Therefore do right by others, and in doing so, you are doing right for yourself. Don't leave *you* out of the equation. I used to work every day of the week, including Saturdays and Sundays. My work consumed me. Then one day I realize that I couldn't do that anymore. It wasn't healthy. I needed some "me time." Too much of anything is not good. I had to eliminate one day out of my work schedule to rest my mind and spend time with my family. I had to get my mind right again and prioritize my life. I began exercising at a local gym. I stopped working late hours and went to bed earlier than usual. I found myself waking up in the morning with more energy than I previously had. For breakfast, lunch, and dinner, I started eating healthier meals. I started drinking healthier drinks, which in turn cut down my sugar intake level in half. I was now well equipped to handle work and personal situations in my life—I highly suggest that to also do right for yourself and take care of your body. Nourish your mind by reading and learning the right things. Get to know the real you. Be happy. Stay positive. Do the right thing! Smile more and get angry less. Be a pleasant person to be around. To get to that positive mental state, some people do yoga. Some people meditate. Some people pray early in the morning. Whatever your thing is, go in a quiet place and have some "you time." Sit there for about ten minutes and don't think about what your day is going to be like. Don't think about yesterday. Don't think about any problems. Just sit there and think about nothing. Blank! Inhale. Exhale. Do that until you don't realize that you are breathing. Practice meditative breathing and one day you will master the art of breathing. Do that every day and you will see a positive change in your life. Then you will be able to attack the world with positivity.

Of course there are pitfalls out there. No one ever said that the road to fulfilling your vision was going to be easy. Sometimes you will say, "Oh! Why me?" Sometimes I sit by myself and just cry. It's not because I'm not man enough to handle the situation, but I get emotional because I fell short of a certain success that I was aiming for and it hurts. But you know what? I never quit! I always end up finishing the race that is set before me because of the way I treat my body. I am in the best shape of my life, and because of that, I am able to run my race without getting tired. Doing the right thing for me enables me to become a winner. No matter your religious or ethnic background, everyone can relate to doing the right thing. I work with people from all around the world, and the one thing I notice is that we all share the same struggle. We all have bills to pay. The only difference is our mentalities. It comes down to you doing the right thing for yourself. But beware; quitting causes the Universe to turn off the light switch to that vision that you are pursuing, and striving to win keeps your vision alive. So I recommend staying on the grind. Don't quit! Make the moves that will guarantee your success. I think people who quit in life are weak because they are not strong-minded. Paul said in 2 Corinthians 12:10, "That's why I take pleasure in my weaknesses, and in the insults, hardships, persecutions, and troubles that I suffer for Christ. For when I am weak, then

I am strong." Wow! What a powerful statement. Later on in Philippians 3:14, Paul goes on to say, "I press on to reach the end of the race and receive the heavenly prize for which God, through Christ Jesus, is calling us." According to Paul, no matter which obstacles came his way, he had his mind made up that he would continue to press forward until he had crossed the finish line into heaven. At his weakest points, he found strength in his faith in Christ Jesus, and that faith was enough to make him strong. Therefore I say to you, to fulfill any positive vision, I highly recommend that you also put on that same perseverance that Paul had in his pursuit of Christ's ultimate vision for the world. Have the same kind of faith that Paul had, and you will finish your race one day and ultimately fulfill that vision that you have pursued for so long. Keep pressing forward. Make no excuses. Be a winner. Compete with yourself and not with others. Set new records by beating your old records. If you did something last year, this year make sure to do that same thing ten times better. Grow by working on your craft every single day. Don't let up. Constantly continue to do the right thing, and the right thing will be done unto you.

Chapter 5

The Grind: Hard Work and Dedication

I remember watching one of the episodes of the Floyd Mayweather, Jr., and Shane Mosley 24/7 series on HBO and was immediately intrigued by a particular slogan chanted by the Mayweather camp. Floyd, walking around the boxing ring like a lion on the prowl, yelled out "hard work!" And in response to these two words, Team Mayweather yelled back, "dedication!" Floyd repeated the words *hard work* four more times, and Team Mayweather replied *dedication* four more times. Then on the television I received a visual of Floyd hitting the speed bag with lightning-fast quickness. His attentiveness was accurate. Floyd, a five-division world champion, winner of ten world titles and two-time Ring Magazine "Fighter of the Year," knows a thing or two about hard work and dedication. When his opponents are rigorously training hard in the gym for a match against him, he is also working hard preparing in the gym for them. But the difference is this: While they are doing three rounds of sparring with only one sparring partner, he is doing six rounds of sparing with six different sparring partners. While they are having one training session a day, he is having three training sessions a day. While they are comfortably asleep in bed, he is punching a heavy bag or running several miles down a deserted street in Las Vegas. Hands down he is one of the hardest working athletes in the world today. There are no shortcuts with him. He trains hard year-round and is in tiptop shape. Every time a referee raises his hand in victory is a testimony to his hard work and dedication.

For Mayweather growing up as a kid in Grand Rapids, Michigan, it was his hard work and dedication to the sport of boxing that got him and his family out of the ghetto. Now a multimillionaire, with everything that he envisioned as a kid, he still manages to remember where he came from. That's why every chance he gets he always shouts out, "hard work and dedication," because he knows that is one of the master keys to his success. I admire that special quality about Floyd. It shows that successful people like him are only successful because of their continuous hard work and dedication in perfecting their crafts. Oprah Winfrey once said, "The big secret in life is that there is no big secret. Whatever your goal, you can get there if you're willing to work." Wow! Imagine if we all worked hard to fulfill our visions? This world would be void of laziness and everyone would be successfully happy. Rihanna, a multiplatinum selling R&B singer, said, "Success for me isn't a destination…it's a journey. Everybody's working to get to the top, but where is the top? It's all about working harder and getting better and moving up and up." According to Rihanna, the harder you work toward something, the better you will get at doing it, and the better you get at doing it will enable you to move up and up the ladder of success if you continue to work hard at your craft. But keep in mind; you have to apply a great deal of hard work and dedication to accomplish anything of great value.

Hard work and dedication—what exactly does that mean? To understand that powerful slogan completely, we have to break it down. It is widely believed that to have expertise in a field such as music requires about 10,000 hours, which is equivalent to about ten years of practicing on your keyboard, drum machine, guitar, etc. If you carefully look at all the hard work and dedication you have put into perfecting your craft, you will notice that you were just being diligent in your pursuit of your goals—the steadfast application or continuous effort put forth by you to accomplish a certain task. Laziness is the opposite of diligence. A lazy person cannot achieve or maintain anything of great value. According to Proverbs 6:6-8, the lazy person should take a lesson from the ants and learn their ways because ants, having no guides, overseer, or someone to rule over them, still manage to work hard every day to gather their food. So if the ants can reach their quotas in gathering food for their harvest, why can't you work hard in perfecting your craft so you can live a better life? I say this because to be diligent you can't hate working hard. You become diligent when you love working hard. You must love hard work. Working hard should be a habit that you practice every day. It should be a part of you. You have to wholeheartedly devote all of your time and energy to work hard in perfecting your craft or fulfilling your vision. There's no other way around it.

Either you develop your talent or let it go to waste. I say develop it and live a developed life. Don't leave your talents or your visions underdeveloped because your life will also become underdeveloped. Develop your craft or vision to your full potential and live a healthy balanced life because of it.

I can honestly say that I got my love and appreciation for hard work from the people closest to me. My parents. My family. My wife. My friends. My neighbors. I saw them all working hard throughout the course of my life. My parents together, as husband and wife after many long years, took a lot of hard work and dedication on their part to remain with each other. No matter what we went through as a family, they worked hard to guarantee that we would remain together. They never let any obstacle interfere with their family vision. Gossip never distracted them. They never abandoned or quit on their vision. Their hard work and dedication gave my sister and me the platform to also pursue and fulfill our visions. I wasn't born with my parents' hard work and dedication. Like everyone else I had to develop the habit of working hard and also had to build up my dedication to work hard by watching people around me who were working hard and dedicated to their chosen vocation.

I remember my father getting up at four o'clock in the morning to go to work. He never complained because he had a vision to fulfill. He could have stayed in bed, but that would have hindered our growth as a family, so he chose not to. Lying comfortably in my bedroom, snuggled under the softest comforter a kid could have, I would sometimes wake up when I heard my father's truck starting up. Then I would go back to sleep, wake up hours later, and start getting ready for school. My father would work all day and exhaustedly come home late in the evening. He would take a shower, eat his dinner, and then plan his next day. I saw him doing that same routine each day. I witnessed that throughout my childhood years. My father was very dedicated to his business and worked hard to support us. Him getting up four in the morning showed us how much he loved and cared about us. Some people might say that they can't or simply won't wake up four in the morning for anything or anyone because that's too early a time for anyone to be waking up. But my father was different. He believed excuses were for quitters. His positive way of thinking subconsciously rubbed off on me in the long run. It's true when people say that children learn by example. When it came down to my schoolwork, everything came easy to me because I took after my father. He didn't make any excuses in his life, and that meant that I couldn't make any excuses in my life. I was getting driven to school. I didn't have to drive. I didn't have bills or a mortgage to pay. My parents provided food, clothing, and shelter for me. All I had to do was to excel in school. That was the quota I had to meet on every report card. So in school I sat in my classes and listened attentively to my teachers. I did my class work and homework without complaining. At home I studied for my tests and passed every one of them with an excellent grade. I did such a great job in imitating my father's hard work and dedication that I became an honor-roll student.

I also saw my mother working hard. She instilled many good traits in my sister and me while our father was out working. Every day after school my duties were to pick up my sister from the bus stop and make something for us to eat. I had to make sure that the floors were all swept and mopped, and I washed all the dirty dishes in the kitchen sink. I made sure that our house was clean before my mother got home from work. Then I had to do my homework. I consistently followed that routine day after day. When I was old enough to work, I realized that I wanted to pursue a career in business. I got my first high school internship in the accounting department of a local business in Deer Park, New York. I worked every day and did my job so well that I went from an intern to being hired. My first paycheck was a testimony to my hard work and dedication. I worked for that company for two years before moving on to another job at a doctor's office. I was happy to be generating my own income, but more important, I was putting myself around successful people that had successful operating businesses. Every chance that I had to show off my hard work and dedication I did so by doing extra work like labeling envelopes or cleaning cabinets. Whatever I had to do, I did more than what was expected of me. In no time, I was rewarded with a pay raise. Seeing that my hard work and dedication had paid off made me to want to work even harder, and I became dedicated to the grind from that point on.

Some might say that their parents weren't good role models; therefore, they couldn't learn by their parents' examples of how to be hard working and dedicated, but instead, they picked up nothing but lazy habits from watching them. For this unfortunate person, I will say take a look around you. I'm sure that you have an aunt, an uncle, grandparents, distant relatives, neighbors, friends, or someone out there that you know who is a hard worker. Someone that loves you enough that wouldn't mind you tagging along with him or her while they are at work. By being around this hard-working and dedicated person, hard work and dedication will eventually rub off on you. As I stated earlier, we all don't have the same starting point in life.

Another person might say that his father abandoned him and his mother was forced to raise him by herself. So growing up, he didn't have a father figure to look up to. For this person I would say this that your mother is a great example of someone who is hard working and dedicated to what's left of your immediate family structure. She didn't quit on your father and her vision of being a responsible parent. No! Not in a million years! When your father deserted his responsibilities and left, your mother didn't break down and get up and leave. No! She didn't abandon you. She stayed by your side and stuck it out with you. When her responsibilities doubled, she had to work two to three jobs to make ends meet and support you. You didn't raise yourself. The food that you eat every day she worked hard for and provided that. The television shows that you watch every day she worked hard, and provided that. The clothes that you wear every day she worked hard, and provided that.

Therefore you should always show your love and appreciation for your mother. Applaud her because she is doing a great job. Everything that you have is a direct result of your mother's hard work and dedication. She is a strong and powerful woman. If she is working two to three jobs, that should at least motivate you to want to do better. You should want to reward your mother by doing something good for her. Make sure that when she comes home the house is clean, there are no dirty dishes in the sink, and the garbage has been taken outside. Things of that nature. Show her your appreciation the best way you know how. I salute all the single mothers and single fathers out there for keeping their visions alive by working hard and staying dedicated to their families.

Hard work and dedication can also be viewed as having a positive mental attitude toward doing a certain task. People have to have that mentality in their minds before they can fulfill anything of great value. Whether it's promoting a new television show, selling a new product to the public, or simply getting a new client, you have to be hard working and dedicated to be successful. Otherwise it won't work. Your lack of devotion to your vocation will cause you to lose whatever it is that you are striving for. You have to be resilient to things that will get in your way. You have to beat the odds to win. But to perform your job the best way you know how means that you have to continuously work at it and be dedicated to it at the same time.

I've been a hard worker my entire life. I love doing what I do because I'm dedicated to it. I'm so devoted that I don't even consider it hard work. That's the mindset that you have to have to become successful. If you want to accomplish something of great value, apply hard work and dedication to that particular task or vision and you will accomplish it. If you have to make a thousand phone calls per day to pitch a brand new product to a thousand potential buyers in your area, then that's what you have to do. You have to be devoted to doing just that one task until you reach your desire goal. You have to say to yourself, I'm going to do it, and I won't quit until I get the job done. If you have to hand out ten thousand flyers within two days to get the word out about your up-and-coming event, then that's what you have to do. If you have to send out a thousand e-mails saying thank you to the people who purchased tickets to your event, then that's what you have to do. Hard work and dedication are all about doing what you have to do to get the job done. There are a lot of people out there who are just sitting around, letting time pass them by, waiting for their big break to land in their laps. Life just doesn't work that way. You get what you put in, and if you're not putting in any hard work, and if you're not dedicated to that hard work that you're putting in, then guess what? You can forget about it. You will not get very far in life, and your visions will all be unfulfilled. Nothing is just going to simply happen for you. You have to get up, get out, and make it happen. You have to believe that you are destined for greatness.

For you who have made up your mind that you are ready to apply hard work and dedication in your life, I would strongly suggest that you get your mind right. Focus on the task that you want to accomplish, and prepare yourself to go after it. Preparation might come through deep meditation, light or heavy exercising, or simply listening to a motivational speaker or inspirational music. Whatever your thing is, do it. Get into your zone. After that step is accomplished, go into your daily planner and see what task has to be completed for that day. If you do not have a planner, I strongly recommend that you purchase one and start prioritizing your days. Planning will help you to fulfill your vision faster and more effectively. Without a plan, you are just drifting aimlessly in life. So get you a planner. Write down all the necessary steps or goals that must be completed before you accomplish your ultimate goal or vision. Each and every day you should have a planned task to perform. I suggest leaving one day out of the week for relaxation purposes. After you have completed a task in your planner, check it off, or simply draw a line through that accomplished goal. Seeing a check mark next to a goal that you have accomplished will motivate you to keep moving forward. Pretty soon you're going to see so many checks in your planner that you might call it your checkbook. But beware; some days you might find it difficult to complete all of your daily tasks. Don't be discouraged because distractions come in many different forms.

You have to use time management to stay focused. Set aside time to work, and set aside time to play. But make sure that you're working at least eight times as many hours as you are playing. Prioritize your time by using your daily planner to its maximum potential. The next step is to set up a deadline or a timeframe stating when you will start working to the desired time that you will stop working. This is very important because too many overtime hours will be detrimental to your overall health in the long run. Work only between those hours that you have chosen to work. Nothing more, nothing less. This will set your pace. After your workday is done, it is done. Do not bring your work home. Go home, enjoy your family, or occupy your time with your favorite pastime. When you wake up the next morning, get back into your work mode and look at your daily planner. Whatever task that needs to be completed for that day, go out there and complete it. Continue this routine every single day until your ultimate vision is fulfilled.

The only difference between an unfulfilled visionary and a successful person who has fulfilled at least one vision is hard work and dedication. The successful person doesn't want to lose, so they put in twice as much work as the person who is accustomed to losing. The successful person is more focused, and they don't let any outside force distract them from reaching their goals. For them, hard work becomes addictive. They found a day and started pursuing their visions from that day forward. Most of them started out working for free as interns in fields that they wanted to pursue, but in due time, because of their hard work and dedication to their vocations, they rose from the basement level to the roof of that company where they interned. For them, there were no boundaries or restrictions that held them from fulfilling their visions. Sooner or later, they became so big that their bosses wanted to partner up with them. These courageous visionaries foresaw their visions and conquered them by working hard, and you too can conquer your visions when you apply hard work and dedication in your life today.

Chapter 6

Making the Dream Work

Walter Percy Chrysler, founder of the Chrysler Corporation, falls under the category of a team player and a good man. According to Proverbs 13:22 KJV of the Bible, it states that "a good man leaves an inheritance to his children's children: and the wealth of the sinner is laid up for the just." The Chrysler Building, an art-deco-styled skyscraper located on the east side of Manhattan, came into existence for this very reason. According to an article written by Roth Piermon - The Silver Spire: How Two Men's Dreams Changed the Skyline of New York; Chrysler is described as wanting the building as a project for his sons, who had suffered the misfortune of growing up rich, and whom he wished for them to feel the wild incentive that burned in him from the time he first watched his father put his hand to the throttle of an engine. Wow! What an incredibly powerful statement and a great motivational example of someone doing right and doing good. Chrysler, one of the wealthiest men in the automobile industry at the time, knew he couldn't accomplish his vision by himself. Therefore, he hired a great architect named William Van Alen to design his vision and put together a team filled with contractors, builders, engineers, building-services experts, and skilled laborers who manually laid down 3,826,000 bricks to complete the building's construction. Now standing at an impressive 1,047 feet, the identifiable and gargantuan Chrysler Building is tangible evidence that proves that the teamwork of Walter Chrysler and his team of like-minded individuals truly led to the fulfillment of Chrysler's vision.

Teamwork is the cooperative effort by the members of a group to achieve a common goal. No one accomplishes anything of great value without the help of others. Without a team you will eventually fail at fulfilling your vision. Vince Lombardi, an NFL hall of fame coach of the Green Bay Packers, said, "Individual commitment to a group effort—that is what makes a team work, a company work, a society work, a civilization work." What an interesting statement. According to Mr. Lombardi, this world would have been running backward if it weren't for teamwork. He would not have won two Super Bowls with the Green Bay Packers if it weren't for teamwork. Apple Inc., Exxon Mobil, McDonalds, and every other major corporation would not have existed if it weren't for teamwork. African civilization, Asian civilization, and Western civilization would not have existed if it weren't for teamwork. So quit trying to do everything by yourself. Surround yourself with a team because teamwork can help you get to your destination faster than you can by yourself. Teamwork minimizes your workload.

Imagine me trying to build the Great Pyramid of Giza by myself. It would be impossible. The Great Pyramid consists of an estimated 2.3 million limestone blocks. How would I perfectly measure and cut all those blocks by myself? Better yet, after miraculously cutting every block, how would I transport them across the river to the construction site? Something to think about isn't it? It is well documented that the largest granite stones weigh anywhere from 25 to 80 tons and were located 500 miles from the construction site. I don't know about you, but growing up I was always great at math. That means if the largest granite stone was 80 tons, what would it be in pounds? If 2000 pounds equals one ton, then 80 tons is equivalent to 160,000 pounds. Wow! Imagine me trying to carry 80 tons by myself. But the Egyptians knew better. They realized that it would take teamwork to complete the construction of the Great Pyramid. It is estimated that tens of thousands of skilled workers constructed the Great Pyramid, and seeing the splendid job that they did should convince anyone that teamwork is the way to go. Maybe you might not need tens of thousands of people's help to reach your desired destination, but a skilled group of people working alongside you can make a huge difference. Remember I said "skilled." The Egyptians used skilled laborers only. There was no room for any error. That's why the Great Pyramid, and everything else that the Egyptians created, always came out perfect. The Egyptians were the first to bring skills to the table. To this day, the Great Pyramid, which was built from 2560 to 2540 BC, and other Egyptian works of art, is still standing tall for the world to see. That's perfection. Therefore, you should always follow the Egyptian's way of doing business: surround yourself with a team of people that are skilled in their chosen field. Otherwise what you're striving to achieve will always come out less than perfect.

Currently at ACA, I can honestly say that I have the most amazing team in the world. I wouldn't replace them for anything because they are hard working and dedicated to reaching our common goal. But sometimes in life, if you make the wrong decision, you will get dealt a bad hand, so choose your teammates very carefully and specifically. Choose them like you're choosing your spouse. If you are a person that cannot adapt to playing different roles, I would highly recommend that you do not work with your buddies that you hang out with. One day your love for them might cloud your better judgment to make an unbiased decision that might hurt you as a businessman. It's always best to keep your friends your friends, your coworkers your coworkers, and your family your family. Separate the three, but like everything else in life, there are a few exceptions to the rule. Some people work perfectly well with their friends and family members. No problems at all. They are like-minded and have one common goal. I work with two of my family members. Our relationship is not always perfect. When we are at work, we take our family caps off and put on our business caps. Our relationship has flourished as a result of that. After work, we take off our business caps and put on our family caps. We have been doing this for years and will be doing it for more years to come. My advice to you is this: Take a good look at what you really want to accomplish. Then take a look at your teammates. Do you see anyone who is out for him or herself? Is there anyone who is just there because of the fame? Is there someone around you only because you have money? Take your time, analyze your surroundings, and truly see people for what they really are.

After identifying those opportunists, gradually distance yourself and your team from them. You will benefit in the long run. I teach everyone at ACA one basic rule—build the business and never chase the money. When you build the business, and it's successful, money will come in abundance. If you chase the money and neglect your business, you will find yourself on the losing end. One question I always ask my client is what would you rather have, a lot of money, or a successful business? The ones that don't take their time to constructively think about the question I ask hastily rush to answer and say that they would rather have a lot of money than a successful business. To them, choosing a lot of money seems like the right thing to do. They could be right. On the other hand, the clients who take their time to consider my question a little bit more always choose having a successful business over having a lot of money because they know that individually they are their businesses. They know that money can come and go. It can be lost or gained with or without a business-minded person or a team managing it. They know that by having a successful business, they also have a successful team, and if they have a successful team, a successful flow of money will come their way.

A famous slogan chanted by activists in the Pan-African Movement is "No Independent Rule!" Edward Blyden, W.E.B. Du Bois, Marcus Garvey, Paul Robeson, Jomo Kenyatta, Kwame Nkrumah, and a host of other leaders understood the fact that teamwork or unifying their powers and working together would be more powerful than each of them having individual powers and working separately. Imagine if Africa became the United Countries of Africa. What do you think would happen? For one, it would put all the countries on that continent on the same team, and together as one, if they work hard and are dedicated to the overall success of their team, they would successfully solve all the problems that are facing Africa today. But no one country can do all of that by themselves. To fulfill a vision that great, they would need the same kind of manpower and teamwork that the Egyptians used to construct the Great Pyramid.

On a team, everyone has to play off each other for the team to be successful. Each person has to understand his or her role. They have to understand their duties and what their purposes are within their respective teams. They have to know what their job descriptions are. Let's say that you're on an NBA basketball team, you are the superstar of the team, and your head coach centers all the attention on you. He runs all the plays your way because you are a proven scorer. Every night on average you drop thirty points, ten rebounds, and eleven assists. You end up breaking the record for the most triple doubles in a season. You feel great about your individual accomplishment and often-times brag about to the dismay of your teammates. But there is one thing that's bothering your fans. Your team didn't make it to the playoffs because your team lost a very close and decisive game. In fact, your team lost the decisive game when you broke the triple-double record. In the locker room, stinking and feeling disgusted, you begin to think to yourself, what could you have done differently to have helped your team advance into the playoffs. Then it finally dawns on you that you had been a selfish player your entire career. Instead of making that one extra pass in that decisive game, which would have tied the game and sent it into overtime, you decided you wanted to win the game by beating the buzzer and hitting a three-point shot. But you missed. You start to think about all the other players on your team that had it in their power to also score, but you were too selfish to pass them the ball. You realize that if you were a team player then your team might have made it into the playoffs. So time passes and next season comes along. You take a deep breath and the first thing you do on the court is pass the ball to a fellow teammate. The second thing you do is pass the ball to another teammate. The third thing you do is to take a charge from an opposing player. Next thing you know your team is up by a wide margin and you didn't even score yet. At the end of the game, you are not rewarded player of the game, but your team won. Now you start to realize the power of teamwork and that it is essential to your team making the playoffs. Then it's halfway through the season and your team has the best record. The fans are yelling their support at every home game. You feel good about yourself because you allowed your teammates to share in the action. You realize that one of your teammates who you thought couldn't shoot to save his life has a better jump shot than you. He is now scoring twenty to thirty points a game and has raised his game to a superstar level. Next thing you know your team is finally in the playoffs for the first time in its brief history. Then you guys beat three seeded teams in a row. Now your team is in the finals. Wow! What an extraordinary story. You look back at what you and your teammates have accomplished, and suddenly you feel a sense of joy that you have never felt before. You are really happy for the first time in your life because you have allowed others to help you fulfill your vision. Your team ends up winning the championship, and you are rewarded most valuable player. To show their love for you, your teammates carry you on their shoulders into the locker room while thousands of satisfied fans are screaming your name at the top of their lungs.

It's been proven time and time again. Successful people will always tell you that they have the greatest team around them. Therefore, the way you assemble your team is very important. You have to be cautious when interviewing future prospects. You have to network to find the right candidate. Once you find that ideal person, you have to be able to delegate, which means you have to be able to transfer authority or responsibility from one person to another. You can't do everything by yourself. You will have to share the workload or work yourself out of the picture. One of the biggest reasons why people don't want a team around them is because they feel they can do everything all by themselves. They don't want to delegate their responsibilities to others, probably fearing that their delegated tasks won't get completed the way they want them to be done. Who knows? But whatever their reasons are for not wanting a team must be reevaluated quickly because everyone has weak points. No person was born with every single gift. For example, let's say I have the gift of promoting people but lack the gift of singing, and you have the gift of singing but lack the gift of promoting yourself. But if we work together as a team, both of our goals will be met. I would promote you to the best of my ability, and you would perform to the best of your ability. Together nothing would be able to stop us. When searching for a new team member, find the area where your company is lacking, and find someone skilled enough to fill that void. If you can't design your company's website, get a graphic designer. If you don't have a PR representative, get a publicist. If talking to people intimidates you, get a talkative and well-liked person to do all your pitching to potential clients. If you can't write to save your life, get a writer. Whatever area it is that you are lacking in, fill it with the right person. Once that individual has been identified, ask them quality questions. What are their visions in life? Where do they see themselves in three to five years? Why did they choose their current profession? Do they currently have a job? Or why did they leave their last job? Ask them for job references. Follow up on those references to make sure that they are legitimate. Find out if they graduated from high school or college. You have to dig deep but not so deep that you are invading their privacy. But to protect yourself, you have to know if this person is dependable or not.

Once your team has been established, keeping them together will be a difficult task. Personalities will clash, and the communication barrier will have to be addressed. Before those things are under your control, you will have to lead by example. You will have to be the best team leader that you can be, but you can't be a dictator when you are instructing your team on what to do. You brought each one of them in for a specific reason, which was to help you reach a certain goal or help you fulfill a particular vision of yours. Therefore, you have to let go of doing everything yourself and let your team do what they were called to do. You have to believe in their abilities to do their job well. When you give them this type of freedom, they will love to come in every day and work for you because you always do right by them. When they complete a certain task, or draw in a big client, reward them by simply saying thank-you or taking them out to lunch every now and then. Do something small to show your appreciation for their hard work and dedication. Also, you must give them the space needed to create. This will be their create space. Since everyone is motivated by money, give them financial incentives or rewards. What I do is have team competitions. I split up my team into two groups, and whoever gets the most clients receive a thousand dollars. This way I win and they win. No one is jealous of anyone because everyone is making money. Also I try my best to talk to each of them nicely. I show them respect, and in return, they also show me respect. I can't take the credit and say that I'm the reason why ACA is successful. The simple fact is that the ACA team made ACA successful. Period! Our teamwork made it happen.

Chapter 7

Education: The Master Key to Unlocking Success

There are three types of education: formal education, self-taught education, and the school of hard knocks education. It is very important that no matter what type of education you are categorized in, you at least have to get a basic formal education, which is simply graduating from high school. There are some people who take it a step further by continuing their education and graduating from college and graduate school: for example, doctors, lawyers, dentists, and school teachers. The second group of people, after getting their formal education, take another route. Instead of going to college, they take destiny in their own hands by educating themselves through reading books or surfing the Internet for information and attending seminars. The successful ones out of this group are usually strong-minded, focused, hardworking, and dedicated individuals. The third group of people probably never graduated from high school, probably never obtained their GEDs. Probably worked at many low-income paying jobs to make ends meet. Nothing came easy for them. Name any bad situation, and they have been through it many times. They didn't receive their education in the classroom but experienced it harshly in the streets during the course of their lives. They usually have occupations that are considered simple. The best among them do extremely well in life because of their common sense and hands-on learning ability.

Anyone who has been educated by all three of these educational genres is truly fortunate. They will excel at anything that they put their minds to. No one educational genre is superior over another. They are all springboards that were designed to assist you in diving into the sea of life. Anyone can fulfill any vision, but without choosing one, you will fail and become an underachiever. Some people fulfill their visions sooner than others, but that's okay. Remember to pace yourself at the learning pace you are comfortable with, and eventually you too will reach your destination.

It is not abnormal for a college student to change his or her major several times during the course of their study. Some end up graduating in a particular discipline, and then turn around and say that they don't want to be whatever it is that they have become anymore. Therefore it is very important, while you are young, that you identify what it is that you want to become. Hold that vision tightly in your mind and see yourself becoming that special person every day until you become that special person. Stand on your word that you will do everything in your power to fulfill that vision of becoming that special person. You are the master key in your life. Only you can unlock your visions and set them free for the world to see. But make sure that the career path that you choose makes you feel fulfilled inside. Do not choose a career that you hate. Pick something that you love doing and do it. Don't just accept the status quo that you have to graduate from college to find a good job to be successful. No! There are plenty of millionaires out there that would tell you that they didn't even go to college or dropped out of college early to pursue their visions full-time. They made sure to at least get a high school education, and I suggest that you do the same thing.

Take Mary Kay Ash, for example. Without a college education or any training in the cosmetic field, she founded her own business, known to the world as Mary Kay, Inc. Because of her drive and knowing what it was that she wanted to do, she did it. Now decades later, nearly half a million women have also started their own Mary Kay businesses by following in her footsteps. Wow! What an extraordinary achievement.

Take another look at another multimillionaire who cut to the chase. Michael Dell, with only a thousand dollars, dropped out of college at the age of nineteen to operate his PC's Limited company, which later became Dell, Inc. He wasted no more time learning subjects that weren't in his field. He knew what he wanted to do and he did it with the knowledge that he had acquired. But everyone's situation is different. That's why you must decide which of the three educational routes you want to take: college, self-taught education, or simply just going out into the world and doing what it is that you do best with the knowledge that you already have.

A few high school basketball players have gone from prep-to-pro, meaning from high school to playing basketball professionally for the NBA. Kobe Bryant, Kevin Garnett, and LeBron James. There wasn't any need for them to do so. They had already blossomed as basketball players so there was no need to test them out on a collegiate level. The NBA saw that they were professionally ready and scooped them up. I believe that once you know what it is that you want to become, then you will also know which educational route you need to take. But no matter which one you take, you will encounter obstacles and challenges.

Your education background sometimes determines who you are. It opens your mind to learn things that hopefully might grab your interest. However, sometimes the connection is not made, and you are not interested in the field that you are studying or working in. You are just buying time or collecting a paycheck so to say. There is no love there. You probably are only doing it because everybody else is doing it. It might be following the trend of going to college. After you have registered for classes, challenges like student loans, depleted savings, or your job laying you off begins to take their toll on you. You start to reconsider the path you have chosen, and you quickly want to push the reset button and start all over again. You start to reevaluate your life. What is it that you really want to do? Most people at this stage of the game get all confuse and make another unfocused decision. They choose another career that they will eventually grow to hate. This frustrating cycle will continue again and again until that individual learns to focus. He or she has to match what it is that they want to become with the best educational route possible to reach their destination. It's as simple as that. You have to propel yourself in the best educational direction that will best meet your visionary needs. Sometimes that means taking matters into your own hands and educating yourself. Malcolm X once said, "Without education, you are not going anywhere in this world," and he is right. Education is very important. It determines if you will or will not accomplish a certain goal or vision. Also, everyone needs to keep learning for the rest of his or her life because as our technological world grows you also have to evolve with it.

By no means am I advocating dropping out of school to pursue your visions. No! I promote formal education a hundred percent. I want you to go to school, learn, and be like Benjamin Carson Sr., an extremely gifted African American neurosurgeon who in 1987 made medical history by being the first surgeon in the world to successfully separate Siamese twins conjoined at the back of the head. He was awarded the Presidential Medal of Freedom, the highest civilian award in the United States. Mr. Carson had to choose the path of formal education because that's what all neurosurgeons are required to do. So instead of reinventing the wheel, he graduated with honors from high school, earned a degree in psychology at Yale University, and attended the University of Michigan Medical School to study neurosurgery. He is truly a great role model and a perfect example of someone who used formal education to his advantage. Life has the strangest ways of educating us. Every day we learn something new. I have a saying that I say seven times every morning. "Every day, in every which way, I learn something new, and because of that I will become better and more educated as a person." This is something you should also say quietly to yourself to help you focus on accomplishing your vision. By repeating that phrase seven times every morning, right after you wake up, you will begin to notice your mind evolving and becoming more knowledgeable. You will become very eager to learn, and your eagerness to learn will carry you in the right direction of learning.

Chapter 8

Patience Is a Virtue

Patience is the positive state of endurance under difficult circumstances; once your state of mind gets negatively influenced, you have lost your patience. Some people call it the art of waiting, and mastering it takes a lot of perseverance through suffering. Not having it means that you will never fulfill any vision of great value. The majority of your decision-making will be made quickly or hastily. You will favor short-term rewards over long-term rewards even though long-term rewards would be more beneficial. You will take every shortcut in life instead of walking the long way. Whenever you see hard work approaching, you will run in the opposite direction. You will want everything immediately. Waiting in line, waiting in a waiting room, or simply waiting for someone to return your phone call will become a major problem for you. You will become uncomfortable when a letter doesn't arrive in your mailbox on time. When someone is running late for justifiable reasons, you will become upset at them. You will favor fast food restaurants over traditional restaurants. When faced with complex obstacles, you will try your best to overcome them, but because you lack patience, you will eventually give up.

Quitting is a sign that someone lacks patience. On the other hand, having patience is truly a virtue. Thomas Jefferson, the principle author of the Declaration of Independence and the third president of the United States, said this regarding patience. "Nothing gives one person so much advantage over another as to remain always cool and unruffled under all circumstances." While others around you are getting frustrated and upset over things that they can't control, there you are, also facing the same calamity as they are but remaining calm. Those that have succumbed to petty worrying will now look up to you because you are in control of your emotions while everything else is falling apart around you. That's the power of having patience. It allows you to be in control of your life, which in turn gives you the ability to handle troubling and uncomfortable situations.

Would you like to be in control of your emotions when you encounter a troubling situation in your life? If so, I would highly recommend practicing patience right now. If you lack patience, I would suggest that you identify one thing that really gets on your nerves. An example could be that you hate the way your mailman positions your mail in the mailbox or you hate the way your spouse talks to you. Whatever that troubling thing is, it gets you upset, and you always lose your temper. Write that troubling thing down. The next time your spouse speaks to you in an undesirable way, you now have a choice to either flip out or calm yourself down. Choose to calm yourself down by taking a deep breath and exhaling. Think about something that you like about your spouse and let that gentle image of him or her empower you to overcome your anger. Ask in a courteous way if he or she could change his or her tone of voice when speaking to you. Then say I love you and walk away. If it happens again the next day, don't get upset. Once again, take a deep breath and exhale. Say again in a nice way that he or she should talk to you correctly. Say I love you again and walk away. What you are basically doing is teaching or training your spouse how to treat you correctly and in return you are developing patience by doing so. Do this every day until your spouse starts treating you right, and when that happens, you will have had patience with that person.

The experience gained from that situation will give you the confidence that you need to control your emotions. You will know that there is a waiting time for every desired result. But to learn that, you first had to plant that seed into your spouse's mind. Then you had to nurture it every day with kind words of appreciation until the seed started growing and establishing its dominance in your spouse's mind. Day after day you saw the cooling effect of its growth in your spouse's changing behavior toward you. Then one joyous day, your spouse begins to address you properly. Even though your seed was metaphorical, you can still be considered a successful spiritual farmer because the intangible seed that you planted in your spouse's mind produced a result called *change*. Farming is an occupation that requires a great deal of patience.

In this Universe, everything that's great is worth the wait. Everything takes time. You have to be patient when you are pursuing your vision or handling a business deal. You have to love playing the waiting game before you get any desired result. You might have the best vision and the best team in the world, but somehow no profit is flowing your way. Don't get upset.

Hold your composure and keep striving. Even though you may be in debt and creditors are knocking on your front door for prompt payment, don't get upset. Hold your composure and keep striving. No matter what troubling or uncomfortable situation you are going through, don't get upset, hold your composure, and keep striving. It's as simple as that. Be patient with the situation like you were patient with your spouse's situation. Know that every successful person has gone through what you are now going through. It's not permanent. You are just passing through it, and because you're just passing through it, there's no reason to lose your temper while you're in it. Look at the bigger picture. The more you continue on your way, the faster it will be for you to make it out of your predicament. Nothing of great value happens without practicing patience.

I have worked with many different comedians, and one thing that I have noticed is that the successful ones have a great deal of patience. They understand that it takes time to build their career; it doesn't happen overnight. They will sometimes do stand-up at a comedy club for as little as twenty-five dollars. Sometimes for free. They will do this every single night until their desired result is accomplished. They work tremendously hard to make us laugh. I have personally met some comedians that would perform at four or five different comedy clubs in a given night. Wow! That's extraordinary. After each of their sets, I would see them network with their audience. They know what it takes to keep their names out there and the buzz growing. They will also work on different projects. They have no problem with being stage warmers for bigger acts. They will do whatever needs to be done for them to build their brand.

One of my favorite comedians who have a lot of patience is Wil Sylvince. He has toured the country with the likes of Damon Wayans, D.L. Hughley, Chris Tucker, and many other notable comics. I love his work ethic. His drive. His passion. I love everything that he represents. Patience is in everything he does, from his delivery on stage to the way he behaves off stage. Deep down he knows that his time is now, and everything that he is doing right now is building up for his one-hour HBO special or his lead role in a Hollywood blockbuster film. His daily grind has won him fans from around the world. I saw his vision when I traveled with him around the country. The many obstacles that he had to overcome were daunting. He faced difficult moments that would have angered the average person, but somehow he held his composure and continued to strive. When he didn't get his desired result, he didn't get aggravated and give up. No! He held his composure and continued to strive. Failure after failure, one let down after another, and being constantly told no didn't discourage him. He took a deep breath, held his composure, and continued to strive. When he stumbled and fell and bruised his body, he didn't stay down. No! He got back up and continued to run his race. There were times when he felt like he had arrived, that the rough times had passed away. Everything in his life was going perfectly well. His career was blossoming. Then setbacks would arise and take his happiness away. But through it all he still managed to hold his composure and continued to strive. Wil's patience is the kind of patience that you will need to fulfill your vision.

When I was a kid, my parents used to teach me patience by not immediately giving me everything that I wanted. They would make me work hard for it. If I behaved and got good grades in school, I was rewarded with the things that I wanted. But most of the time after I had lived up to my end of the bargain, I would forget all about what I had asked for. That discipline showed me that for everything asked for there is a waiting period. That's life. Starting out, you shouldn't try for homeruns. If they come, they come. Focus on hitting the ball. Your main objective is to get on base and eventually score. In the process of doing that, be patient, and wait for the next pitch. But be very careful; life is very tricky. One second it will throw you a curve ball and the next a fastball. You will never know what pitches she will throw at you, but don't get upset if you swing and miss. Every successful person has strikes against him or her. Just hold your composure and prepare to swing again. This time life might throw you another strike, but remember again to hold your composure and prepare for the next pitch. At this point, being patient will empower you to maintain that focus needed to swing at the right pitch. So there you are, firm in your batting stance, and life throws you a pitch outside of the strike zone. But you didn't swing because swinging for it would have surely struck you out. Another pitch is thrown outside of the strike zone and you wisely didn't swing at it. You remained patient again. Then life throws you a changeup right down the middle with the intent of striking you out, and you hit the ball out of the park. Fans are screaming your name. While you are rounding the bases and coming home, you hear a small voice within you saying, "I told you patience is a virtue!"

Concluding Words by
Jean Alerte

I want to say thank-you to all you visionaries out there that took your valuable time to read this book. My purpose is to unleash your inner vision, bring it out to the forefront of your mind, and then show you the different master keys to achieving them. Nothing comes easy in life, but I firmly believe that if you always do right, and make the right decisions, your rough roads to success will be smoothed considerably. Remember winners never quit and quitters never win. So keep on striving until you reach your desired destination. I hope you enjoyed reading this book. I hope it inspired you to always do right. I hope it inspired you to pursue your vision. You only have one life to live, so why not live it to its fullest potential? This is your time. Take care and God bless.

Jean Alerte Thirtieth Birthday

For my thirtieth birthday, my wife and I sailed the Mediterranean on the exquisite Norwegian Jade cruise ship. We visited Egypt and its pyramids, Israel, Cyprus, Rome, and several sophisticated cities in Europe. The beautiful landscapes intrigued us both as we traveled from port to port along several eye-catching coastlines. The sea fascinated me the most. I compared it to life, and our cruise ship I compared to an aspiring individual en route to fulfill his or her vision. Although our ship was vast in size, it was still extremely small in comparison to the size of the sea. One thing that I observed at the end of our trip was that the entire cruise was not a smooth ride. Sometimes the water was calm, and at other times it was rough. But no matter what the emotions and moods of the sea were, our captain still managed to safely navigate us through the calm and rough times until we reached our destinations. To me he is a great representation of that responsible and persistent drive within us to continue on until our goals are met. It goes to show that the road we are traveling on in life is not an easy one. At times it will be smooth, and at other times it will be rough.

Don't surrender when faced with temporary obstacles. Be triumphant. Exercise that true courage within you to weather any storm that may come your way. No problem or roadblock is too big or strong to prevent you from fulfilling your vision.

By continuously adding persistence to your efforts, you will see the dark clouds fading away and giving room for the sun to shine its guiding light in your life.

About Jean Alerte

Jean Alerte was born in Port Au Prince, Haiti. At the tender age of five, he migrated to Brooklyn, New York. His work experiences range from being a licensed mortgage banker, a marketer and manager of extraordinary, talented individuals, a brander, and a consultant to many businesses and industry professionals. Jean was awarded the Young, Gifted & Black Entrepreneurial Strategic Marketing Award in 2012. He has produced numerous comedy concerts and tours, and his long list of accomplishments have landed his company, Alerte, Carter, and Associates, accounts with many A-listed companies and entertainers. Jean serves as the Vice Chair and Chair of the Fundraising Committee for Egypt Cares Family Foundation. He currently resides in Queens, New York, with his wife. Jean and his wife recently opened Brooklyn Swirl a Frozen Yogurt Shop in the heart of Stuyvesant Heights, Brooklyn. *Do Right, Do Good* is his first book.

To know more about Jean Alerte, please visit his website at www.DoRightDoGood.com or contact him via e-mail at Jean@dorightdogood.com

About Zangba Thomson

Zangba Thomson was born in Bong Mines, Liberia, West Africa. At the tender age of eight, he migrated to Jamaica, Queens, New York, and after years of experiencing life in the urban underbelly, he rose academically and studied Journalism and Creative Writing at York College. He acquired a decade worth of knowledgeable wealth in the realms of spirituality and metaphysics. He is the chief executive officer at Bong Mines Entertainment LLC and lives comfortably with his family in Baldwin, New York. His debut novel is titled *Three Black Boys: The Authorized Version*.

To find out more about Zangba Thomson, please visit his website at www.bongminesentertainment.com or contact him via e-mail at Zangba@bongminesentertainment.com

Acknowledgments

Jean Alerte: I would like to thank God for the visions that he gave me. My faith in you turned those visions into reality; my wife Gayna, thank you for being my partner, my best friend, and I appreciate your heart and positive spirit. We are going to make history with Brooklyn Swirl; my parents, I want to thank the both of you for your sacrifices and for giving me the best life possible. I am very grateful for everything you two have done for me; my sister Stephanie, thanks for always being a great sister; my parents-in-law Denise Dunn and Sam Samuel, you guys are the best and I love being your son; my aunt Marie Vincent and Uncle Eddie Vincent, I appreciate everything you've done for me; Uncle Bouby, Tatie Gina, Tatie Dominique and Uncle Patrick thank you for being the first to give me a chance, Tatie Sheila, Ninnin Yamilee, all my cousins, aunts and uncles, My ACA team and family, Tamar Bazin for being the best partner and true inspiration to so many, My partners and brothers Jonathan Sykes & Jason Sykes for sharing the vision and having faith, Jennifer Cadet I appreciate all that you do and thanks for being part of the team, Lyvio Gay, Dalia Jackson, Gina Williams, Kanayo Ebi, Kemar Cohen, Metkel Hailu, Courtanie Sanders, Sandrine Charles, Daniela Frasca, Shaniqua Hargett, Tori Jackson, Eric Dussek, Melissa Reyes, Mechell "Big Meech" Turner, Patrick Knight, Chauncey Glenn, Jessica

Alvarado, Ishmael Abrobwa, and everyone that worked with ACA in the past.

I appreciate everyone's continued support. Thanks to Zangba Thomson for helping me with this project; Keon Bryce of Soulfoke Music Inc for the best track we made history brother, thanks to Alvina Alston for being there throughout the entire project and for being such a positive individual; thanks to Mark O'Mard for being a true friend that meeting in the city changed everything "Thank you Mark", Robert Flower words can't express my appreciation for you brother, you're a true inspiration, JoAnn Monroe we moving sis thanks for being in my life, Robert Standfast, Cuba for many years of great designs and many late nights, Kyle Donovan of NV Magazine, Debra Lewis, Onyinye Akujuo we did it, Paul Rosen, Rudy Renelique, Randall Thomas for being the best student and friend congrats again to you and Cathy, Perry Cadet and family, All the loan officers that worked with me at Dynamic Mortgage Bankers, Frank Gateau congrats on following your vision and thank you for our friendship since O.L.R, Jickael Bazin for inspiring me and showing me the power of residuals "ACA Communications" look forward to more morning talks and mentoring others, My little cousin Anais Bazin remember always to follow your dreams and have fun, Delano Imran & Sue Tsai I appreciate our partnership and friendship, Laurence Covington for always supporting me and you are the next great one, Theresa O'Neal, Ash Cash my brother we are going to make a difference, Don Ross, Geoffrey Pope thanks for opening the door, the New York Giants, Les Pines thanks for being there for me, Beau Carter, Alexis Diaz, CB, Paul Basist "Can't Un-ring a bell", Wil Sylvince, Shaun B. Laurent, Michael Skolnik for your continued support and thank you for making my year sir,

Chris Nassif, Dimitri Logothetis and family, Anthony Gurino and entire family, Kevin Hart for giving me the opportunity in 2009 that opened so many doors, Nate Smith for the tough love but we family, Jason Stone for believing, your integrity also for being the greatest mentor in the touring industry, Heather Federlin, Dan Kellachan, Mike Bertowitz for believing, Tony Rock, Dwight Elmore, Capone, Mark Viera, J. Alexander Martin, Shawn "Pecas" Costner of Def Jam, Jeffrey Gurian, Gavin and Cheryl "Salt" Wray, Amber King, Tommy Rebello, Phill Hammond and Raymond Dean the GetAppMe.com guys you guys are going to change the game, Malachi Wilson for everything I appreciate all the knowledge "J5 the protégé" is now the teacher, Eric from Avalon, Sam Marelli for mentoring Gayna and I, Patrick Jeffrey for everything "Major Deals" and my Godson Aaron Patrick stay focused on your dreams and always dream big, Toya Patrick, DJ Fa-Delf & Egypt power couple thank you for being there since day one and congrats on baby girl, Valerie Geller, Craig Davis, Dr.Fanel Alerte and family, Dwayne Byfield thanks for keeping me fresh, Rudy and Mackenzie Kimbro-Vincent for being there and all the support, Latasha Johnson, Tabitha of Desi Lu Sweets, Mike Feller (CPA) and family for your continued support and all your knowledge, Lisa Thorne and Mommy Thorne congrats, Latrice Lyde, Khaleel & Kamarie Keep Going and never stop, Mark Baker, Jemaine Buchanan, Otis Guy, Troy Bigs, Steve Suydam (Benz dealer), Nandina Lawson, Isa Elayyan, Rashaad Lawson, Clifford Gray, Andre Vice, Rhamon Belfrom, Mike Horry, Nathan Gregory, Troy Whitfield, Jr. Johnson, Dulani Brock and The Entire ABM Family, Jennifer Coulombe, Dolores Machuca-Ruiz, Tamara Ehlin, Will Benson, Mrs. Perry-Eising, Mrs. Nancy Binger, DPHS Friends and Teachers, Peter Brooks and Lisa Patalano of

Schenck USA thank you for everything you showed me when I was a intern, the interns at OBT who made me move Richard Gutierrez, Barry Crute, Will Thomas, Sandy Oliver for all your support and prayers & Justine Uncle Jean will always have your back so stay focused on your vision, Andrew Brint (CPA), Ernie DeMarco, Parnell from whatspoppin.net, Robin Kearse, Shawn A.K.A Mims, Marie "Mamoune" Jones, Todd Duncan for "Time Traps" that aided my development, David Baptiste for the great artwork, Bang for understanding me and not letting me settle. Book cover is hot!, Outer Focus for the photo shoots you really captured my vision, Aggie and Reginald "Picture Perfect" Vincent, Richard Vincent, Chris Laraque, Mark Jean, Ishmel & Tosh for great production and Tosh for the best book trailer, GetAppMe.com for the great website and mobile app, Michael Most, Paul Anthony of Full Force for being a champion and keeping it sexy, Greg Selg (Wealth Advisor) We got Power brother, Pastor A.R. Bernard (My Pastor), my mentors from a distance, Sean Combs "I'm Locked In", Will Smith, Shawn Carter, Floyd Mayweather Jr., President Barack Obama for proving that change is possible, Russell Simmons, thank you for writing Do You: that book made me evolve into a better businessman. I appreciate your support and kind words. I am truly humbled by everything, Dr. Dennis Kimbro for showing me that anything is possible when you believe, you're a true inspiration and thank you for being part of this project and the words of wisdom, Chris Gardner, thanks for sharing your story with the world, and I am glad that I am able to share this with you; thanks to everyone that I crossed paths with and everyone who supported my growth!

Zangba Thomson: Hotep to The Most High The Highest Yahuwa, YHWH, for giving me Right Knowledge, Right

Wisdom, and Right Overstanding to co-write a book of this magnitude, Yashua, for his spiritual guidance and soulful teachings, my family, the staff at Bong Mines Entertainment LLC, my friends, everyone who has ever contributed to my success, and Mr. Jean Alerte, thanks for allowing me on board to help you deliver this timely message to the world. Hotep!

Gayna Alerte and Jean Alerte

Stephanie Alerte, Marie Alerte, Joseph Alerte and Jean Alerte

Denise Dunn, Jean Alerte, Gayna Alerte, Sam Samuel

Amourelle Donnay, Jonathan Sykes, Tamar Bazin, Kemar Cohen, Melissa Dondele, Frank Gateau, Jason Sykes, Dalia Jackson, Lyvio Gay, Jickael Bazin, Jean Alerte, Cherie Samuels take a picture after first meeting in ACA's office in Williamsburg, Brooklyn

JoAnn Monroe, Jean Alerte and Rob Flower attend seminar in New York City

*Gayna Alerte, Jean Alerte, Michael "DJ Fa-Delf"
Jackson and Tiana "Egypt" Sherrod.*

Jason Sykes (ACA), Jean Alerte, Paul Anthony (Full Force),
Pastor A.R. Bernard (Christian Cultural Center),
Frank Gateau (Julian Casimir Jewelry) and Bowlegged Lou
(Full Force) at Brooklyn Borough Hall. Full Force & Reverend A.R.
Bernard were honored with a Proclamation for almost 30 years of
achievement, community service representing Brooklyn New York

Jean Alerte and Patrick Jeffrey at a screening of Buffalo Soldiers in Harlem, New York in 2010

Alvina Alston and Jean Alerte

Kevin Hart and Jean Alerte hanging out during the taping of the commercial for Jean's first major comedy show which was headlined by Kevin.

Chris Nassif (CEO of Diverse Talent Agency), Dimitri Logothetis(Producer) and Jean Alerte are celebrating getting his first client Anthony Gurino (Actor) signed to Diverse Talent Agency in October 2009. Diverse Talent is the number 9 talent agency in the country.

Get App Me Boys Frank Gateau, Phill Hammond, Jean Alerte, Raymond Deane

*Robert Standfast and Jean Alerte enjoy a
great day of golf in the fall of 2011*

THE ONLY THING MORE PRECIOUS THAN A DIAMOND IS A LIFE.

THE
LIFE
BRACELET

In 2012 alone, more than 575,000 Americans are expected to die from cancer. It is a disease that affects and touches nearly every single human being. Sue Tsai & Julian Casimir & Co have created a one of a kind bracelet to benefit the American Cancer Society that captures the beauty and value of the precious gift we call life. The LIFE bracelet III, part of the LUX collection is made up of grade A Amethyst with 14k rose gold. With your purchase of this bracelet, you along with the American Cancer Society can help save lives and create a world with less cancer and more birthdays. Starting March 1st, 2012, LUX will contribute $20 of the sale of each LIFE bracelet III to benefit the American Cancer Society. For more information on our partnership please visit www.BraceletsForLife.com. With your assistance, we can help people stay well and get well, find cures, and fight back because when it comes down to it the only thing more precious than a diamond, is a LIFE.

 THE OFFICIAL SPONSOR OF BIRTHDAYS.®

The American Cancer Society does not endorse any product or service.

The LIFE Bracelet was created by Julian Casimir Jewelry and Sue Tsai to benefit the American Cancer Society. Jean Alerte supports LIFE.
www.braceletsforlife.com

Made in the USA
Charleston, SC
28 August 2012